Faith Beyond
The Good, the Bad and the Ugly

A Story of Redemption

Julio Cesar Moncada Paladino
(Nickname Cocacola)

Faith Beyond the Good, the Bad and the Ugly

A Story of Redemption

Author: **Julio Cesar Moncada Paladino**

Design and Layout: Ysmerio Rodriguez

Publisher **Branded Lives**

ISBN: **978-1-962388-31-3**

Copyright Notice

No part of this work may be reproduced, stored in a retrieval system, or transmitted in any form or by any means—electronic, mechanical, photocopying, recording, or otherwise—without the prior, express, and written permission of the copyright holder.

The use, extraction, reproduction, or transformation of this work, in whole or in part, for the purpose of training, feeding, or developing artificial intelligence (AI) systems, language models, or automated machine learning technologies is expressly prohibited without the explicit consent of the author or copyright owner.

Any violation of these rights may constitute an offense against intellectual property, subject to penalties under applicable U.S. law, specifically **Title 17 of the United States Code**, as well as under international treaties such as the **Berne Convention for the Protection of Literary and Artistic Works and the TRIPS Agreement** (Agreement on Trade-Related Aspects of Intellectual Property Rights).

For authorized use requests, educational or corporate licenses, or reproduction of excerpts under legal terms, please contact the author or publisher through official channels.

All rights reserved. © 2025 Julio Cesar Moncada Paladino

ABSTRACT

January 1, 2025 marks the beginning of a new year. Last November (2024), I turned sixty-nine… and the fire's still burning! I'm finally taking on something I've long postponed in my life: writing a book.

I first wanted to do it back in 1986, but my boss and friend, **Edgar Vargas Guzmán**, advised me not to. He was right—it was far too early to start writing my story. But now that I've made up my mind to do it, I'm not quite sure where to begin. I feel like the opening line of that famous sonnet by the great Spanish poet **Lope de Vega**—what a bold move this is!

Still, I gave it a try: I wrote a sonnet dedicated to the working man, an ode to my mother, and a few short pieces I drafted between 1965 and 1975.

I've decided to divide this book into three clear parts. Its title, The Good, the Bad, and the Ugly, is not meant to echo the cowboy movie, but rather to present my unfiltered confessions—though not quite like those of Saint Augustine.

The Good—because good things are the blessings God has prepared for me and still gives me, though I don't deserve them, and the good deeds I've managed to do (few as they may be compared to the bad ones).

The Bad—because the bad includes my mistakes, the wrong things I've done and don't wish to repeat in order to remain in God's grace, the misfortunes I've faced, and the harmful actions of others that have affected me.

The Ugly—because the ugly stands for everything that is neither one nor the other: the lukewarm, the ambiguous, the things that somehow got tangled up in my life along the way.

I began writing this book thinking it would be an autobiography—but in truth, it isn't. It's more like a collection of wanderings, not told in chronological order, but in a light and sometimes scattered style, to keep the reader curious and eager to reach the end.

It's not easy to fit a whole life into just a few pages; yet a story written like a novel—a true-life novel—can be fun to read. I hope these opening reflections help the reader understand what this so-called writer (me, who really isn't one) wants to convey in these pages.

There's so much to write about that, as I said before, the best approach is to give a summary of life—not a never-ending book. So I'll try to tell this tale with simplicity and honesty: the events and ups and downs of this novel-like autobiography. Well then, here we go… let's see how it turns out.

Still, what will always matter most is the reader's response—their acceptance and opinion. The foundation of that acceptance lies in critique, analysis, review, and evaluation of the work. So, I sincerely hope it will be well received.

Ode to My Mother Isabel Paladino.

Name of Her Majesty,
surname of a subject,
name of a saint,
ally of all that is good.

Sonnet to the Good Worker

How joyful the mornings rise,
thoughtful and cruel in their labor,
belonging to the one who wears them beneath his robes,
with sweat, with honey, and with toil's flavor.

You live forever walking through the fields,
with an uncertain, unknowing fate,
and while you stumble, fall, and yield,
another stands tall and celebrates.

Time will wash your footprints away,
the wind will dry the sweat from your brow,
yet deep within your chest will stay
the memory of labor's vow.
And triumph, after every blow,
will be the prize your soul will know.

Dedication

To my devoted wife, **Ana Patricia Ramírez León.**

To my wise children: **Nellys Patricia, Braxis Isabel, María Lais, Julio César, Gonzalo Josué, Bryan David,** and **César Ricardo**.

To my friends, who have walked beside me all my life.

To my enemies—because without them, I wouldn't have learned how to defend myself.

To my relatives, for they carry my blood.

To my grandparents and parents, because through them, I came to be.

To my siblings: **Elizabeth, Miguel Eduardo, and Javier Emilio**, my companion in youth.

And to everyone else—a brotherly embrace.

Contents

PART I THE GOOD
Chapter 1 Deogracias Moncada — 17
Chapter 2 Julia Cuaresma — 25
Chapter 3 Paladino-Cabrera — 29
Chapter 4 My Father — 33
Chapter 5 My Mother — 39
Chapter 5.1 The New Shoes — 43
Chapter 5.2 My Mother's Legacy — 45
Chapter 6 Me: The Best of the Good — 47
Chapter 6.1 Leaving Nicaragua — 51
Chapter 6.2 José Luis Howay — 53
Chapter 6.3 The Sugar Mills — 57
Chapter 6.4 The UCA — 59
Chapter 6.5 Early School Years - In Love, Maybe? — 63
Chapter 6.6 Starting High School — 67
Chapter 6.7 University Years — 73
Chapter 6.8 Adventures — 77
Chapter 6.9 My Birth — 81
Chapter 6.10 In Love — 83
Chapter 6.11 Athlete — 87
Chapter 6.12
Here and There: My Mentor, Dr. Jaime Downing — 91
Chapter 6.13 Professional Relationships — 95
Chapter 6.14 Thanks Be to God: El Trapiche — 99
Chapter 6.15 Grateful Friends — 103
Chapter 6.16 First Job in the United States — 107
Chapter 6.17:
Trip to Nicaragua and Return to the U.S. with My Family — 111
Chapter 6.18: Church Work and Travels — 117

Chapter 6.19 Patricia, the Lovely Girl	119
Chapter 6.20 My Father and Mother in Laws	123
Chapter 6.21 Friends in My Golden Years	127

PART II: THE BAD

Chapter 1 Nightmares	131
Chapter 2: Hiding Out	133
Chapter 3: The Papaturro Tree	135
Chapter 4: Intolerant and Disrespectful	137
Chapter 5 The Waterfront	141
Chapter 6 The Insurgent	143
Chapter 7 Testing, Testing	147
Chapter 8 High School Graduation – Passion	149
Chapter 9 The Consequence of Liquor	151
Chapter 10 The Sale of My House	153
Chapter 11 In Prison	155
Chapter 12 The Theft	161
Chapter 13 Peter and USCIS	163
Chapter 14 My Retirement	167
Chapter 15 My Free Time	169
Chapter 16	
A Few Things I Did in My Free Time	171
Chapter 17:	
My Left Knee	175

PARTE III THE UGLY

Chapter 1 White Boots	181
Chapter 2 Encounter with Dina	183
Chapter 3 My Grandfather's House	185
Chapter 4 ATCHEMCO	187
Chapter 5 Renting Homes	189
Chapter 6 Buying Cars	191
Epilogue	193

PART I
THE GOOD

(My Grandparents, the Moncada Cuaresma Family)

My paternal great-grandparents were **Santiago Moncada and Gloria Reyes.**

My paternal grandparents were **Pablo Deogracias Moncada Reyes and Ana Julia Cuaresma Hernández**.

On my grandmother Julia's side, my maternal great-grandparents were **Emiliano Cuaresma and Eulalia Hernández.**

That's as far as I can trace my lineage on the Moncada side; beyond that, I simply don't know.

Exposición de Artes, Industrias y Oficios

Departamento de Masaya

El Comité de la Exposición Departamental de Artes, Industrias y Oficios

Considerando:

Que el trabajo inteligente del hombre aplicado al poder productivo de la tierra, a las energías naturales; y en general al desarrollo de la riqueza y perfeccionamiento de las Industrias, Ciencias, Artes y Servicios, es fundamento de la prosperidad, independencia económica y política de los pueblos;

Considerando:

Que la diversificación de las industrias, origina mayor demanda de trabajo y eleva los salarios a sus justos términos; que el mercado nacional debe ser el primero en abrir sus puertas al producto nacional para estimular y proteger la producción interior; y siendo un deber patriótico despertar las fuerzas latentes de nuestro país de las cuales es una revista la presente Exposición.

Por Tanto:

En vista del dictamen del Gran Jurado Calificador, se confiere a la sección de *Sn. Droguerías Mexicanas* el presente **Diploma** de *Honor* por los trabajos de *Sus Inventos Musicales*.

Dado en el Palacio de la Exposición a los *treinta* días del mes de *Enero* de 1930.

MINISTRO DE FOMENTO

JURADO — JURADO
JURADO — JURADO
PRESIDENTE — SECRETARIO
DIRECTOR GENERAL — TESORERO

EXPOSICIÓN DE ARTES
E INDUSTRIAS
DEPARTAMENTO DE MASAYA

Chapter 1
Deogracias Moncada

It's worth telling that my grandfather, Pablo Deogracias Moncada Reyes, served in the Volunteer Army of Nicaragua's Liberal Party during the presidency of General José Santos Zelaya (1853–1919), who governed from July 25, 1893, to December 21, 1909.

My grandfather served under General Juan Escamilla. I still have a copy of a document signed by him. Colonel Moncada was wounded in the Battle of Namasigüe, Honduras, in March of 1907. While he was hospitalized, he received a handwritten telegram from President Zelaya himself (I still have that, too), along with a gift: a ceremonial sword, finely crafted, which he wore with his formal military uniform—*the levita*—adorned with medals and decorations.

That sword, along with four others he had used in his campaigns, was later passed down to his son, my father, Miguel Moncada. My siblings—Elizabeth, Miguel, Javier, and I—used to play with them as if they were toys. Imagine that! We played war with real swords. Laughing and shouting, we'd yell, *"Grab your swords!"* and then came the *click, click, click* of metal clashing as if we were in a real battlefield.

Until one day, my father found out about our dangerous game. He had no choice but to get rid of the swords—he sold them to our neighbor, Dr. Miguel Porta Caldera. I still remember that enormous backyard where we used to play: a huge plot filled with cedar, sapodilla, avocado, and guava trees, and most famously, the *papaturro*—a small, white, sweet fruit. Fallen branches, tall grass up to our chests, the smell of soil—it was a child's paradise. Every kid in the neighborhood came over to play and eat papaturros.

One day, while we were playing, we heard our father's voice calling us. We froze. He walked into the yard, machete in hand, and one by one gave each of us a good whack on the backside. That was the end of that game!

Years later, during the Sandinista war against Somoza (1979)—by then I was already a Chemical-Industrial Engineer from UCA—I saw those same swords displayed in Dr. Porta's living room, crossed like a coat of arms. I didn't say a word, not to his son Miguel, nor to my own father. The cycle had closed. Only the ceremonial sword remained at home, carefully stored away and never touched again.

My grandfather left behind many stories. In 1929, he served as Secretary of the Court Martial, which judged deserters and soldiers from General Augusto C. Sandino's National Sovereignty Army. He was also the uncle of General José María Moncada Tapia, a former president of Nicaragua.

My father was the only child my grandfather had with my grandmother Ana Julia Cuaresma, though in truth they had three other children who died shortly after birth. So, when my father was born, my grandfather said, *"Leave him on the floor; if he's going to die like the others, let him die right away."* But my father lived. I've often thought that I don't have many Moncada relatives—but as for the Paladinos, there are plenty!

I lived with my grandparents, the Moncada-Cuaresma couple, until their deaths. My grandfather, however, had four children outside of his marriage. Before he died, he contacted them, brought them to Masaya, and gave them part of his inheritance. The only one I remember by name was Domingo.

Another story he used to tell: he once lived in the city of León—where some of those children were born—"like a prince," as he said. He worked at Los Prío Restaurant, a famous place in its day, frequented by the great poet Rubén Darío, known as the "Father of Modernism" and "Prince of the Spanish Language." My grandfather, being a true *nica*, used to drink with him.

I also recall that one Good Friday, returning from Lake Granada (Cocibolca), the police arrested my uncle by marriage, Armando Altamirano, for reckless driving and took him to the Masaya jail. When my grandfather found out, he put on his military uniform, holstered his pistol, and went himself to get him out. Case closed.

Another story, told by my grandmother Julia (the reason I was named Julio): one day, my grandfather was sitting outside his house when a man named Justiniano rode by on horseback. He was an enemy of my grandfather's for having served under Sandino. Justiniano tried to charge him with the horse, but my grandmother ran out with a revolver in her hand and shouted, "*If you take one more step with that horse, you'll die right here.*" The man turned his horse and fled.

My grandfather was also a master woodworker, awarded in Masaya for the quality of the guitars he made. He also crafted an excellent homemade compuesto—a liqueur made by mixing spirits with fruit. He drank three shots a day: one before breakfast, one at noon, and one with dinner. "*Two fingers,*" he'd say—measuring the space between his index and little finger.

He was born in San Marcos, Carazo, on January 25, 1877, and died on June 8, 1968, at his home in Masaya, at the age of 91. A strong-willed man, a soldier to the core, I used to serve as his walking stick and altar boy when he went to the market. "Let's go to the market," he'd say, dressed in his formal uniform, revolver at his side, felt hat on his head.

He kept newspapers and journals that told of his military exploits, along with a life insurance policy worth over $30,000 at the time (today, roughly $300,000). Yet when he died, he received no condolences from his party or the National Army. My father, enraged, gathered all his journals and that insurance policy—and burned them. I was twelve years old.

It's worth noting, though, that thanks to my mother, my grandfather received a lifetime pension from the government and the Liberal Party, which later passed to my grandmother Julia. She managed to secure it through her connections with Doña Lía Plata de Hueck and Dr. Cornelio Hueck, who was right-hand man to President Anastasio Somoza Debayle.

From a young age, I was the one who went to collect that pension at Dr. Hueck's house—sometimes even stepping into his bedroom and private office. More than once, I'd run into the politicians of that era there—some of them conservatives, his rivals—gathered in lively debates about the country's politics.

San Lorenzo de la Pabona, abril 25 de 1921.

La Presente Sirbe para dar á manifestar que el Coronel Deograsias Moncada. amilitado en mis fuerzas de Voluntarios desde el 17 de febrero. asta el 25 de abril se a portado ala. altura de su Deber. y hoy le conseso permiso para Reconsentirse asu. domisilio que e en masalla. areglar asuntos interesantes.

Suplico alas Autoridades militares y Cibiles que tengan en cuenta los Serbisios de Dicho por. tador dela Presente.

El Jefe de Voluntarios
Fra[n]. Anilla

TELÉGRAFOS NACIONALES DE NICARAGUA

No. 5

Depositado en Campamento á las 8 p.m. del 8 enero de 1907
Recibido en León á las 9 p.m. del ... de 190...

A Diogracias Mercado

J. Emilio Guerrero, Silvio Gallegos, Bernardino Rizo Landero,
Lázaro José Hernández y demás
firmantes Hospital de Sangre.
Con verdadero interés he leído
su expresivo telégrama en que hacen
presente una protesta de adhesión y
simpatías hacia el Gobierno que
yo presido y su patriotismo
por la causa que defiende Mi
campaña en los campos de Honduras, Creame Udes. que me sien-
to orgulloso de ser el Jefe de una
nación que cuenta con hijos...

El Telegrafista

TELÉGRAFOS NACIONALES DE NICARAGUA

No. ...

Depositado en ... á las ... del ... de 190...
Recibido en León á las ... del ... de 190...

A

tan valientes y gue... hacen del pa-
triotis... una virtud en...
elevasá... el mas alto grado.
Los triunfos que han obtenido
las armas nicaragüenses en
la cruzada contra el Gobierno
de Honduras, se deben al heroi-
co arrojo de Udes. Estan-
dome en mi solo la honra
de la dirección de la Guerra y
hubiera podido consumar... la
victoria. Vivan... que pueden...
que estan Udes. satisfechos de
la asistencia que reciben...

El Telegrafista

Telégrafos Nacionales de Nicaragua

No. _____ Ch. _____

Depositado en _____ á las _____ del __/__ de 190_
Recibido en León á las _____ del __/3__ de 190_

A

en esa Centro y amigos es ver-
dad que el Gobierno de Ud.
ya sé que y siempre hasta el
reformado su gobierno sigue en
defensa de la patria y de las
instituciones liberales, siempre (¿?) nosotros tambien
es cierto que los nobles jamas
de León con su filantropía
de siempre contribuyen muchi-
simos a dulcificar _____ la
penosa situacion de Modesto Cordero
_____ el atento saludo que
me hacen y mis votos

El Telegrafista

Telégrafos Nacionales de Nicaragua

No. _____ Ch. _____

Depositado en _____ á las _____ del __/__ de 190_
Recibido en León á las _____ del __/3__ de 190_

A

por pronto restablecimiento
Jefe y amigo
Zelaya

El Telegrafista

A. Somoza D.
GENERAL DE DIVISION G. N.

CORRESPONDENCIA PARTICULAR

MANAGUA, D. N., NIC.

Abril 26 de 1966

Coronel (MD) G.N.
Egberto Bermudez,
Médico Director Hospital Militar,
Managua, D. N.

Muy estimado Coronel:

    Permítome presentarle el caso del señor Deogracias Moncada R., viejo Soldado del 93 y fiel amigo del Ejército y de nuestra causa, a quien el suscrito vería con muy particular agrado el que sea internado en ese Hospital para efecto de que se le practique operación en la vista al mismo tiempo de que se le suministre la medicamentación necesaria.

    La generosa atención de Ud. en este caso será altamente agradecida, mientras aprovecho la ocasión para repetirme de Ud.

Muy atentamente,

A. SOMOZA D.
GENERAL DE DIVISION G.N.

ASD/dmo:

Juan B. Sacasa
Presidente de la República de Nicaragua.

Saluda a su amigo don Deogracias Moncada y le manifiesta que tuvo el gusto de recibir su apreciable de 3 del corriente mes de cuyos conceptos tomó nota y se impuso de su solicitud, la que tendrá en cuenta para tratar de complacerlo.

Managua, 4 de Mayo de 1933.

Chapter 2
Julia Cuaresma

MMy grandmother, Ana Julia Cuaresma de Moncada—that's how married women used to identify themselves back then, with the "de" to signify belonging, though today that might seem inappropriate—was a wise woman, like so many grandmothers are: strong but gentle, intelligent though not formally educated. In short, an exemplary grandmother.

She was born on February 11, 1899, in Nindirí, and died in Masaya on September 18, 1990, also at the age of ninety-one, just like my grandfather.

My father was what we used to call a *"milk brother"* to Camilo Frech, a well-known merchant in Masaya. That term was used for children who were nursed by a woman other than their biological mother. After giving birth to my father, my grandmother had plenty of milk, so she shared it with baby Camilo.

My grandmother also raised another child, whom she named Emilio, perhaps in memory of her brother of the same name, who had died years before. When he grew up, Emilio returned to visit her and thank her for the kindness she had shown him.

During the 1960s, Nicaragua was in great political turmoil—and as a young man, I wasn't completely detached from it. I remember in 1968, the newspaper La Prensa, directed by Pedro Joaquín Chamorro Cardenal, a vocal opponent of the Somoza regime, published the slogan "¡Basta ya!" ("Enough is enough!") alongside the image of an open hand. I used that same gesture to ask my grandmother for fifty centavos: ten centavos for each open finger. With that money, I'd buy myself a roll with cheese from the street vendors outside the Teatro González. It became, in a way, a "rent" I collected from my grandmother.

When I was in my fourth year of high school, I joined the school marching band. I played the snare drum with a pair of wooden drumsticks, their tips reinforced with plastic to keep them from breaking. But one day—snap!—one broke clean in half. Panic set in; I had no idea how to explain it to the band captain or the school principal.

My grandmother Julia, seeing my distress, asked what had happened. I told her, and she said calmly:

"Hand me the sticks. I'll make a glue that'll leave them better than new."

Hopeful, I handed her the broken pieces. She took a large chunk of cheese, added a bit of water, and set it over low heat on her improvised stove—a half barrel filled with beach sand, supported by four black lava stones from the Masaya Volcano, which we called *"burned stones."*

After two rounds of washing the cheese, she obtained a liquid that looked like whey. On the third, she mixed it with what remained of the cheese, stirring it by hand. She spread that mixture over the broken ends of the drumstick, joined them together, and instructed me:

"Leave them alone. Don't touch them until tomorrow afternoon—they'll be ready."

I did as told. And sure enough, the next day they were sturdier than before! I tried to separate them, but it was impossible; they could break somewhere else, but never at the joint. To finish, my grandmother sanded the area lightly with fine paper to smooth the mark. Perfect. My dear Grandma Julia had just saved me from big trouble at school.

Many years later, I finally understood the secret behind that "glue." During my Chemical Engineering studies, I learned that cheese contains casein, a milk protein that, when mixed with fats and minerals, serves as a base for making adhesives. Later, when I worked as a representative for Kativo de Nicaragua, a company that sold industrial glues, my theory was confirmed. Maybe—just maybe—my calling as a chemical engineer began with that homemade lesson from my grandmother.

Her glue did have one flaw, though: it stank! But it worked. She had learned the recipe from my grandfather, who was also a woodworker and used it to assemble guitars.

Chemists and alchemists, all of us in the family, wouldn't you say??

Chapter 3
Paladino-Cabrera

(My Grandparents, the Paladino Cabrera Family)

My maternal great-grandparents were Eduardo Paladino and Úrsula Cabrera. My maternal grandparents were Eduardo Paladino Guadamuz and María Cabrera.

Both of them were from Granada. My grandfather Eduardo was a dark-skinned man, his complexion tanned by years under the sun—a hardworking merchant who managed to give his ten children a stable life. My grandmother María, on the other hand, was fair, beautiful, and proud, with an unshakable drive for self-improvement that she passed on to her children.

It was with the Paladino family that I was closest, since my paternal grandparents had only one son. My mother was the eldest of the Paladino siblings.

The ten children of my grandparents were:

- Isabel (my mother), married to Miguel Moncada Cuaresma.

- Juana, affectionately called *Mamatía* by everyone. She never married.

- Eduardo, a well-known doctor and Conservative politician, married to Lila Sánchez (Lilita) of Masatepe.

- Armando, the cheerful uncle, a great storyteller and a skilled administrator. He was the general manager of the famous *Ferretería*

Gallo y Villa and one of the top salesmen at Nabisco Cristal, the cookie factory in Managua. Married to Susana Marcos.

- María Jesús (Aunt Mayu), the first to pass away. She was married to Armando Altamirano, who worked at the prestigious Gadala María textile factory in Managua.

- Carmen, who emigrated to the United States thanks to my Aunt Jenny. She married Sócrates Pérez Arévalo from Diriá, Granada.

- Margarita (Aunt Negra), married—and perhaps later divorced—from Carlos Soto of Chinandega, a good man.

- Orlando (Uncle Negro), very smart and lucky—he actually won the lottery! He was married to Teresa Gutiérrez.

- Emilio, a dentist, professor, and dean of the Faculty of Dentistry at the National Autonomous University of Mexico (UNAM). Married to Luz María Arango.

- Teresa (Aunt Tita), married and later divorced from Carlos Reyes, who went to study in Spain. She worked at *La Prensa and El Nuevo Diario.*

From this large Paladino clan came countless cousins: two Paladino–Marcos, five Paladino–Sánchez, one Pérez–Paladino, six Altamirano–Paladino, two Soto–Paladino, four Paladino–Gutiérrez, two Paladino–Arango, one Reyes–Paladino, and the four of us Moncada–Paladino. And that doesn't even include the children from second marriages. Altogether—so many cousins that I've lost count. As we like to say, *"I've got Paladino cousins enough to fill the sea—like grains of sand."*

My uncle Orlando, when he won the lottery, paid for an entire semester of my university studies. I'll always be grateful for that.

My uncle Armando, the joyful one, used to pick me up in Masaya to take me to the university in Managua. He worked for Nabisco Cristal, and even though he lived in Rivas, he'd stop by daily to visit my mother, his eldest sister. My uncle Eduardo, the doctor, cured me of a severe case of ringworm on my scalp. My aunt Margarita, la Negra, always called me by my full name—*Julio César*—and somehow, in her voice, it sounded special.

And my aunt Tita, hardworking and sharp-tongued, used to say with a bit of irony, *"Now what did this boy get himself into?"*

I also remember my grandfather Eduardo well. I used to serve as his walking stick and guide. He liked to put his elegant hat on me, and at bedtime, I'd listen to him pray, naming every member of the family one by one. But there was one thing—he ground his teeth in his sleep! (laughs).

He once owned a large general store in Ticuantepe, up on the plateau of the Masaya Volcano. In his later years, he went to live with my uncle Eduardo in Matagalpa, where he eventually passed away. My grandmother María died earlier. I still remember when we met her at the airport—she was ill and in a wheelchair after a fall in the bathroom. My uncle Eduardo took her to Matagalpa so both grandparents could spend their last days together. And so it happened: first she went, then he followed.

Despite having ten children, my grandparents ended up living apart. He moved to Ticuantepe, and she to Managua, in the San Antonio neighborhood. They never divorced, nor did they remarry. He had a few passing romances; she lived with *Mamatía and Aunt Carmen,* both unmarried, along with the Pichardo sisters, María and Margarita, whom she raised as her own.

In 1960, Mamatía emigrated to the United States. The following year, my grandmother María and Aunt Carmen did the same. At first,

Faith Beyond the Good, the Bad and the Ugly

they lived together, but when Carmen married Sócrates Pérez, they moved to their own place in San Francisco, California.

Every time my grandmother returned to Nicaragua for vacation, she stayed at our house, with her eldest daughter—my mother. Thanks to her, we discovered Monopoly, learned to eat corn flakes, pancakes, Spam ham, and the sweet cookies she loved to dip in coffee with milk.

My grandmother María had a strong personality—one of those women who truly embodied the saying, "When she set her eye on something, she hit the mark." She had an uncanny instinct for sensing what was coming, a gift she passed down to many of her children, grandchildren, and great-grandchildren.

She also had a beautiful cat named Cacreco. When she emigrated to the United States, my mother brought the cat home to live with us.

Chapter 4
My Father

My father—the one God chose for me—Miguel Jerónimo Moncada Cuaresma, was deeply proud of his father, Colonel Pablo Deogracias Moncada Reyes.

As a young man, he worked as a radio operator at La Fundadora Estate in Jinotega, owned by then–President General Anastasio Somoza García. He also served as a radio operator and second in command aboard the famous Nicaraguan ships that sailed the Great Lake of Nicaragua: the *Victoria and the Somoza* steamers.

My father used to woo Miss Isabel Paladino Cabrera—my mother—riding the fine horses from La Fundadora. After finishing high school, Miguel Moncada Cuaresma became a passionate autodidact and avid reader—a man who seemed to know something about everything. Naturally, he bought us many encyclopedias—Barsa and *Lo Sé Todo*, the best of their time—and later donated several volumes to the elementary school at the National Institute of Masaya, then called Anexo al INMA.

Every Sunday, after the 8 a.m. Mass at San Jerónimo Church—celebrated by Father Rodolfo Hernández, who also gave my brother Javier and me our First Communion—my uncle Armando had a surprise waiting for us: a big box full of toy soldiers, ambulances, and police cars with flashing lights. After church, my father would serve a delicious breakfast, complete with his famous *ranch-style scrambled eggs*. Absolutely delicious.

Faith Beyond the Good, the Bad and the Ugly

Trains and Journeys

Some weekends, my father took us by train—on the Ferrocarril del Pacífico de Nicaragua (FPN)—from Masaya to Diriamba to visit his parents, my grandparents Deogracias and Julia. The railway passed through a tunnel before emerging over the slopes of the Laguna de Apoyo, a breathtaking view. Passing through Masatepe, almost side by side with the home of former President José María Moncada, my father would mention that he was the son of the president's uncle—but I never thought much of it. Years later, at UCA, I met one of his grandsons, José Omar. We never identified ourselves as relatives (though my brother Miguel told me he once did).

In Diriamba, we visited the Santa Cecilia Distillery, owned by the Rodríguez Blen family, where my grandfather worked as head of security. His contract included a home on the property. I remember the massive vats of molasses fermenting into alcohol, surrounded by coffee plants and hedges of piñuela. Beautiful countryside.

My father also took us by train to Corinto, Nicaragua's main Pacific port. I remember crossing the famous *Paso Caballos* railroad bridge—wooden pilings over the sea, the train creeping forward inch by inch. Some claimed the line once connected all the way to *San Juan del Sur,* though no train ever reached that port.

In 1990, under the government of Violeta Barrios de Chamorro, the railroad lines were dismantled and sold—an entire mode of travel lost forever. Years later, while worki ng in Nicaragua's sugar mills, I visited the FPN foundry, where they made machinery for the mills. Two others served us as well: *Taller La Perla*, owned by Juan Peters, and another near *Mercado Oriental.*

Faith, Home, and Music

My father was born, raised, and married in the Catholic faith in Masaya, but in 1968 he converted to Mormonism. I never really knew how or why. He was a learned, intelligent man. My mother told him, *"The only Mormon in this house will be you; don't you dare touch my children—or me."* And so it was: the only Mormon at home.

In time, the foreign Mormon missionaries—mostly from the U.S. and Guatemala—became friends with my mother and asked to rent a room from her. They saved money; she earned a little income. A good deal for everyone. If my father hadn't converted, that opportunity never would've come, and my mother wouldn't have had that much-needed extra income.

When the missionaries were out, I—rather mischievously—used their high-quality headphones to listen to their tapes: *Déjà Vu* by Crosby, Stills, Nash & Young; Catch Bull at Four by Cat Stevens, and *Wild World*. Beautiful music.

Work, Justice, and the National Palace

My father worked tirelessly to provide for us and to give us the best he could. A few stories stand out:

- He was Head of Personnel at INCA (National Industry of Nails and Wires, Masaya). Out of a sense of social justice, he raised the workers' wages on his own initiative—earning their respect and the owner's anger. He was fired.

- He was a founding employee at *Cervecería El Águila* in Managua, serving as warehouse and dispatch manager.

- He later worked as warehouse chief at *Puerto Sandino*, on the Pacific coast.

- And eventually at the General Revenue Office in the National Palace.

That last job holds some of my fondest memories. Once a week, we drew straws to see who'd get to go with him to the Palace. He'd hide two matchsticks in his fist—one short (winner), one long (loser)—pressed between his fingers so we couldn't tell. Finally, one day, I won!

I must've been around eight or ten. I played at my father's desk, met his coworkers, and explored every floor. The building was imposing: massive wooden doors, grand halls, marble columns, two guards of honor at the entrance and two more at the staircase. We climbed to the roof, overlooking Lake Xolotlán (Lake Managua), the Campo de Marte, Roosevelt Avenue, Club Managua, and the Central Park with its great fountain and sunbathing lizards. What a memory!

Thirty years later, I returned to the Palace to process my alcohol production permit for my distillery (a story I'll tell later in this pseudo-novel). That childhood view stayed vivid in my mind. Thirteen years after that, Edén Pastora ("Comandante Cero") led the Sandinista commando that famously took the National Palace.

Inheritance, Backyards, and a Lion with Fur

When my grandfather distributed his estate among his children in León, he had already given my father the house where I was born—right next to his own. He also told my father to take whatever portion of the backyard he wanted, since he planned to sell the rest to Candelario González, husband of Violeta Hernández, my grandmother Julia's niece.

Thus, the property shrank from a quarter manzana (roughly a city block, 100×100 meters) to half of that—losing forever the vast, beautiful yard where we once ran and played with swords.

One day, we got into a rock fight with the kids from the back lot. The commotion was so bad that my father, furious, threw a stone that hit a tree—right next to where the neighbors' father was hiding. Minutes later, the man came over to complain. Maybe that was why my father decided against keeping the part of the property that bordered their yard.

That place still lives in my heart. My dear friend and brother, Dr. Gerardo Sánchez, reminded me of it when I visited him in Masaya in 2023.

We had chow-chow dogs, descended from a pair once gifted by General Somoza to a neighbor. Ours was named Milán—pink tongue, red-brown fur, a mane like a lion's. And he truly looked the part. Loyal, smart, and protective, he was family. My mother loved him deeply. When he died at fifteen, she refused to have him thrown out, as was customary then. She buried him in the backyard.

Milán had two male pups: one identical to him and another jet black, with a dark tongue like his canine grandfather's. My father gave them away. We hid them, but he had already given his word. That was that. We cried.

Once, while playing outside with Milán—I must've been about eight or ten—he jumped on my back, knocking me into the gutter. I hit my left eyebrow, split it open, and bled a lot. My mother stopped the bleeding with cotton and alcohol. The scar near my eye remains to this day—a lifelong souvenir of my beloved Milán.

Baseball, Umpires, and a Farewell

My father took us to the old Masaya Stadium to watch the amateur baseball finals between *San Fernando (Masaya) and Flor de Caña (Chinandega)*. The famous Masayan slow-ball pitcher *"Mamá Moncha"* was on the mound. They lost.

Faith Beyond the Good, the Bad and the Ugly

I remember Manuel Tejada, one of the best home-plate umpires. My father introduced me to him after a professional game in Granada between *Oriental* (my team) and *Boer* (from the capital). He asked me, "Who's going to win the championship—the Oriental or the Boer?" I froze and blurted out, "The Boer." Then quickly corrected myself: "No, no—the Oriental!" He laughed and said, "May the best team win."

Another umpire I remember was a tall blond nicknamed *"Chele"*, who would call strikes and strikeouts lifting his right leg and making an elaborate gesture—his own style. I must've been five to eight years old. Those were the days of Nicaragua's beloved professional league.

In 2009, on Father's Day, as he was leaving his Mormon service in *El Rosario, Carazo*, my father was fatally struck by a minibus driven by a drunk man. I mourned him quietly here, in the United States. I couldn't go back to Nicaragua—I was in the middle of my immigration process, and my attorney, Dr. Mario Lovo, advised me not to travel.

Chapter 5
My Mother

Writing—or even speaking—about my mother tightens my throat… and I think my brothers and sister feel the same. To write about her is like trying to keep even the wind from touching a flower, so as not to hide its beauty. Beauty in every sense: an excellent daughter, sister, friend, sweetheart, wife, and… an extraordinary MOTHER!

Thank God for blessing us with such a remarkable woman as our mother. We, her children—Elizabeth, Miguel, Javier, and Julio—were truly blessed to have her.

Goodbye, Chabelita.

Goodbye, Cha.

Goodbye, Doña Chabelita.

Goodbye, Doña Cha.

"Doña Cha, I've got this problem… what do you think I should do?"

That was the endless parade of greetings, of people who came looking for her, trusting her counsel, and honoring her wisdom.

I used to say, *"Mom, buy me a motorcycle! I already have the helmet and the leather jacket my friend Marlon Solís gave me—all I'm missing is the bike. Come on, buy it for me!"*

Smiling, she would reply, "All right, go see Don Felipe Ruiz and tell him I said to make you one—I'll pay him later."

Don Felipe, the master carpenter from the San Jerónimo neighborhood in Masaya, of course never built motorcycles. That was her tender way of saying no.

I'd insist, "Mom, seriously, buy it for me!" And she'd laugh and say, "Hold on, let me go to the backyard and cut some lemon leaves."

That was her joking way of talking about money—referring to the big lemon tree in the yard, tall, lush, and generous, always heavy with fruit all year long, right behind my parents' room.

My mother once ran a large grocery store. Over the years, as she got older, she scaled it down to a small corner shop, selling the daily essentials. There was always money in the house. Sometimes we'd sneak a little to pay for parties at the club or to treat ourselves. But my mother knew everything. No one could fool her..

Stories About Mom

Once, my brother Javier was invited by Pompeyo Porta to go hunting. Everyone brought their own rifle. Javier took the pellet gun our parents had bought for us. He didn't shoot anything that day and, frustrated, slammed the rifle against the ground, cracking the wooden stock.

When he got home, he told Mom it had fallen on a rock. She looked him straight in the eye and asked,

"No, tell me the truth... you smashed that rifle against the ground, didn't you?"

Javier, pale and silent, lowered his head and whispered,

"Yes, Mom... that's what happened."

What hurt him most wasn't the scolding—it was being found out.

Another time, my father came home from work. The moment he stepped inside, my mother said,

"You lost your job, didn't you? What happened?"

Surprised, my father answered,

"Yes… I lost it. I'll tell you later."

My mother had inherited that gift from my grandmother María—she somehow knew things before anyone told her, as if she sensed them. It wasn't fortune-telling or superstition; it was a spiritual gift, one of those seven gifts given by the Holy Spirit.

Chapter 5.1
The New Shoes

¡There's so much to tell about Isabel Paladino, and every story about her is a good one!

One ordinary day, we went swimming at the Salesian School pool in the Monimbó neighborhood of Masaya. We went as a group—my brother Javier, our neighbor Jimmy Moreno Palacios, my best friend Gerardo Sánchez Vega, his brothers, and a few more. We were quite the gang.

In the locker room, I left my clothes and my brand-new leather shoes, freshly bought at Don Agustín Castro's shoe store, *Moda Elegante*. Don Agustín was a friend of my father—a respected and well-known man in Masaya, and a former baseball player for the San Fernando team.

I changed into my swim trunks, and off we went into the pool. Dozens of kids and teenagers were there, paying just a few centavos to swim under the watchful eyes of the Salesian priests. Nothing unusual.

Late in the afternoon, after hours of swimming, we decided to head home, get cleaned up, and later go out with girlfriends or friends. I walked into the locker room to get dressed and… my shoes? Gone! They'd been stolen!

In their place, I found a pair of old, torn, dirty rubber shoes—*Sandak* brand. How thoughtful of the thief! It seemed he'd felt bad about leaving me barefoot and decided to leave behind the pair he no longer wanted.

Faith Beyond the Good, the Bad and the Ugly

From my house in the San Jerónimo neighborhood to the Salesian School in Monimbó was about three kilometers. Can you imagine, dear reader, how I felt—walking almost all of Masaya in those broken rubber shoes, weighed down with guilt for losing my new ones? My mother had warned me: *"Don't wear those—go in sneakers instead."* But no, I wanted to show off my new shoes, to look stylish and proud.

Oh, Mom! What was I going to tell her when I got home?

To make things worse, around that time a litter of puppies had just been born at home—same breed as the ones I mentioned before—and they still hadn't opened their eyes. My brother Javier broke the news first:

"Julio got his new shoes stolen at the Salesian pool!"

"What?!" my mother exclaimed. *"I told you not to wear those shoes, like if you didn't have any others!"*

My mother never hit us. She just said,

"Go to the back room and don't come out. That's your punishment."

I went, head down and tail between my legs, crying over my lost shoes. But being a child, a little while later I wandered back and asked innocently,

"Mom, have the puppies opened their eyes yet?"

She shot back, with that sharp wit of hers,

"You should've opened your eyes, so they wouldn't steal your shoes!"

From that day on, my brother Javier never stopped teasing me with that line:

"Hey Julio, have the puppies opened their eyes yet?"

And to this day... he still does.

Chapter 5.2
My Mother's Legacy

My beloved mother was born on June 8, 1917, and passed away from lung cancer on February 4, 1980, at the early age of sixty-three.

She always told us, *"Study, get a degree, finish university. That's the inheritance I leave you."* And she truly sacrificed herself to make that dream come true—to see her children become professionals.

And guess what? She did it!

Not only did she achieve it—she lived long enough to see us graduate.

- Elizabeth, Executive Secretary, graduate of the Isabel de Robleto School of Commerce (my godmother's institution).

- Miguel Eduardo and Javier Emilio, both dentists, graduates of the *National Autonomous University of Mexico* (UNAM).

- And me, Chemical-Industrial Engineer, graduate of the Central American University (UCA), San Ignacio de Loyola, in Managua, run by Jesuit priests.

That was her greatest legacy: the desire to grow, to rise above one's circumstances.

In her youth, my mother helped my uncle Eduardo study medicine, and he, in turn, helped my uncle Emilio, who went on to study in Mexico. A true chain of siblings bound by solidarity and love—living proof of the spirit of support and unity that my mother planted in our family.

Chapter 6
Me: The Best of the Good

Since we're in the Good section, I'll begin this chapter by saying—with confidence and gratitude—that the best thing that ever happened to me in life is the person God gave me as my wife and companion: Ana Patricia Ramírez León.

We were married on January 25, 1986, but oh, my goodness—the journey we went through to reach that day! Part of that story, I'll save for the *Ugly* section.

Another of my greatest achievements was graduating as a Chemical-Industrial Engineer from the respected Central American University (UCA)—highly regarded throughout Latin America—and doing so while my mother was still alive, a source of pride for both of us.

The University Marathon

My graduation truly was a marathon. Let me explain: I finished high school in 1973 and entered the university in February 1974, starting with the Basic Cycle—the first two years when all students take the same general courses. Then, in the third year, everyone chooses a major: Engineering, Humanities, or Agriculture.

During my general studies, I took *Basic Math* (known as "Math Zero"). I began university as if I were still in high school—carefree, playful, not taking it seriously. The result was predictable: I barely passed my classes with grades of 6 and 7 out of 10, and I failed *Math Zero*.

That failure woke me up. I thought to myself, *"Is this what I really want? Is this what my mother expects of me?"* Without passing that course, I couldn't move on to Math I, and since all math classes depended on that foundation, my degree could stretch to seven or eight years.

I had already decided to study Chemical Engineering, because my father had once dreamed of becoming a chemical engineer but never had the chance. I wanted to honor him. Yet I hadn't started on the right foot—in high school I'd barely passed Chemistry with 7.52 and Physics with 7.51, the minimum to get by, thanks to my own irresponsibility.

Eventually, I came to my senses. My classmates were ahead of me; they'd finish in the normal five years and enjoy summer vacations. I, on the other hand, didn't get a single summer off.

But by God's grace, every subject that had held me back was offered in summer school. So, I took two classes each summer—ten in total over five years—passing them all with grades of 9 and 10. My final GPA rose to 8. Incredible! I graduated alongside classmates who had never failed a course.

I proved to myself that where there's a will, there's a way.

I became the top student in Organic Chemistry, taught by the late Dr. Jaime Downing Urtecho, Dean of the School of Engineering and founder of the Chemical-Industrial Engineering program. Later, he would become my boss in the industry.

I ranked among the best students in the program. It was five years without rest or vacation—but I did it! I missed—well, traded—four years of Masaya's San Jerónimo Festival and countless nights with friends, but I achieved my goal.

My best friend Gerardo was, at that time, studying medicine in León.

My Children, My Pride

Of course, the best of the good also includes my children—my greatest pride.

With Patricia, I had six: Nellys Patricia, Braxis Isabel, María Lais, Julio César Jr., Gonzalo Josué, and Bryan David (the youngest, born in the United States). I also have César Ricardo, who was born long before I met Patricia.

Thank God, they all chose the right path and became professionals:

- César Ricardo, M.A. in Hotel and Tourism Management.
- Nellys Patricia, Ophthalmologist Technician.
- Braxis Isabel, Bachelor in Health Administration.
- María Lais, Radiology Technician.
- Julio César Jr., Business Administrator.
- Gonzalo Josué, Automotive Parts Technician.
- Bryan David, Barber at B. Cutz Studio.

When people ask if all my children are from the same mother, I always reply with a smile:

"Yes—every one of them made with the same one." Got it?

At Okeelanta, the Cuban engineer Lima used to joke that having six kids was far too many—since in his culture, most families only had two. I'd just smile, proud and thankful..

Chapter 6.1
Leaving Nicaragua

Before leaving Nandaime, Nicaragua, for the United States, we gathered as a family to pray, Bible in hand. When the prayer ended, we asked the Lord to give us a word. We opened the Scriptures and, placing our finger on the page, found the passage the Holy Spirit had inspired for us—a confirmation that it was indeed God sending us into exile.

Patricia also placed another sign in God's hands: *"If the china cabinet sells, it will be the Lord's will that we go."* The cabinet was a large piece made of fine laurel wood, with glass doors. When we returned from the U.S. Consulate in Managua—where we had gone to process visas for Gonzalo and Julio, who didn't have them because they hadn't yet been born during our earlier trips in 1991 and 1992—the housekeeper greeted us saying:

"Doña Patricia, the china cabinet's been sold!"

That was it. Decision made. We were leaving Nicaragua.

We traveled to the United States with five children. Nellys, the oldest, was twelve; Gonzalo, the youngest, only twenty-three months—just shy of two years old. As Patricia liked to say, "We're like a little marimba band," or as others teased, "a parade of ducklings." Father John Mericantante Palladino affectionately called our family *"La Escuelita"*—"The Little School."

Father John gave me a letter of introduction addressed to Engineer Ricardo Lima, general manager of the Okeelanta Sugar Mill, which

I mentioned earlier. That letter was the key that opened the doors to that great company. Engineer Lima always supported me.

In Nicaragua, friends and relatives told us we were crazy:

"You won't last past the arrancada in the U.S."

That Nicaraguan expression means, "You won't even make it past the starting line." They couldn't imagine us lasting a month abroad—especially with five young children.

But to keep this book from turning into a marathon, I'll summarize it this way:

Twenty-five years after arriving in this great country, I worked at the Okeelanta Sugar Mill in South Bay, Florida, for eighteen years as a production supervisor—drawing on my earlier experience in sugar mills across several countries.

And during those eighteen years in Okeelanta, every one of my children graduated from college.

If that's what it means to be crazy—then yes, we're crazy: crazy with joy, gratitude, and faith in the God who helped us move forward… to dream—and to live—the American dream.

Chapter 6.2
José Luis Howay

Ah! Speaking of sugar mills—how did I end up working in Nicaragua's sugar industry?

In November 1982, I joined the Javier Guerra Báez Sugar Mill (formerly Ingenio Amalia) in Nandaime—Patricia's hometown, in the department of Granada. There, I was hired as Industrial Director, or Production Manager, sometimes called Factory Superintendent. And it was there, in that very place, that Patricia struck my heart like an arrow.

But let's take it one step at a time.

Before that, I had already been working in Nicaragua's private industrial sector, even before graduating. My most recent position had been as Production Manager at Química Borden Centroamericana until October 1982, when I was just twenty-six years old. I had first joined the company as assistant to the production manager at the invitation of Engineer José Luis Howay, who held that position at the time. When he later moved to the United States, he left me in charge as Production Manager.

José Luis wasn't only my boss—he was also my teacher. He taught Unit Operations during my fifth year of Chemical Engineering and served as advisor for my graduation thesis.

Why did he come looking for me in mid-1981, when I was working in the offices of MIDINRA (Ministry of Agricultural Development and Agrarian Reform) as manager of the Cassava Industrialization Project? There, I oversaw the production of ethyl alcohol for automotive fuel and represented the Central American Institute for Industrial Research and Technology (ICAITI). Our office was right near the Los Gauchos restaurant in Managua.

Back in 1980, when I worked at *Polímeros Centroamericanos (POLYCASA)*, Dr. Jaime Downing (whom I mentioned earlier) had recruited Engineer Howay to return to ATCHEMCO, a chemical company on Nicaragua's Atlantic Coast. That plant was, at the time, one of only three of its kind in the entire world.

ATCHEMCO produced pine oil, *turpentine, dipentene, gensol, longifolene, and light-colored* resins extracted from pine tree trunks—highly useful materials for various manufacturing industries.

José Luis knew those processes intimately, having worked there before. I, for my part, had written my graduation thesis about that very plant, which inspired me to follow him to the Atlantic Coast.

After a year, José Luis had to return to Managua for personal reasons, leaving the company behind. Before leaving, he told me,

"I'm leaving you in charge as Plant Manager of ATCHEMCO."

It was a high-ranking position with an excellent salary. But I replied,

"José Luis, I came here because of you—and because you were my thesis advisor. If you're leaving, I'm leaving too."

With that decision, I showed him my respect, admiration, and friendship. And for that reason, later on, he sought me out again and brought me into Química Borden.

He was an excellent teacher and boss—just like Dr. Downing. I believe that gesture of loyalty forged a lifelong bond between us. José Luis never stopped keeping in touch, and I never stopped remembering him with gratitude.

Years later, both in Nicaragua and in the United States, we met a few more times. Until one day, his wife Margarita called me with the sad news: José Luis had passed away.

May he rest in peace, my dear friend.

Chapter 6.3
The Sugar Mills

The Javier Guerra Sugar Mill was the place where I grew and flourished technically in a truly extraordinary—almost unbelievable—way.

After finishing my contract with Química Borden, I arrived at the mill on November 20, 1982, to take up the position of Industrial Director, recommended by José Bárcenas, who at that time was assistant to Commander Jaime Wheelock Román, Minister of *MIDINRA*. I had once taught Bárcenas in the Chemistry lab at UCA.

At Javier Guerra, I put my knowledge, skill, and experience to the test—and the results spoke for themselves. We achieved the highest sugar production in the mill's history up to that point: 536,000 quintals of refined sugar.

News of this accomplishment reached Mr. Alberto McGregor, son-in-law of Don Gonzalo Benard, the mill's former owner when it was still called *Ingenio Amalia*, before the Sandinista Revolution. Years later, I ran into Don Alberto at the Managua airport, and he and his wife personally congratulated me for the work I had done at their beloved mill.

My Journey in the Sugar Industry

To summarize my 36-year career in the national and international sugar industry:

- I redesigned and modernized production equipment with excellent results.

- We achieved record efficiency levels in every harvest season I participated in.
- I transformed steam boilers and multiple-effect evaporators.
- I improved and replaced juice clarifiers.
- I discovered new methods of sugar production that saved hundreds of millions of dollars.

And it was the same story at every mill where I worked—in Nicaragua, Cuba, and Honduras.

Of course, results like those didn't come without challenges: I made plenty of enemies along the way.

My friend and advisor at the Javier Guerra mill, Engineer Guillermo Ramírez (may he rest in peace), used to tell me:

"Engineer, sugar mills are like cockfighting arenas—every rooster comes in armed to take down the other."

Was he right? Perhaps. They called him Pitusín, and in his time, he even improved the recipe for the famous Flor de Caña Rum..

May 1984, Sugar mill Javier Guerra signing the Sack N° 500,000 of the Sugar Season 1983-1984 reaching a record never equalized

Chapter 6.4
The UCA

EIn 1978, the year I graduated, a reporter from La Prensa came to the UCA. In January of that year, Dr. Pedro Joaquín Chamorro Cardenal—the renowned journalist and owner of the paper—was assassinated. The reporter asked me:

"What's your opinion about the assassination of Dr. Pedro Joaquín Chamorro?"

I answered:

"This assassination will be the spark that drives the Nicaraguan people into the streets against Somoza, and the FSLN (Sandinista National Liberation Front) will seize the moment."

And that's exactly what happened. I took part in the occupation of the UCA, which I'll talk about in *The Bad*.

Oh—and I almost forgot: I played first-division soccer with the UCA for a couple of matches, against CONARCA and América. (I'll tell you more later.)

Back in high school, it was obvious I was more quick-witted than studious—too playful, treating school like a sport. I had to take summer school after a low final grade in Physics in my fourth year; when I sat for the makeup exam, I aced it. That's how it should've gone all year—but no, I spent my time *birdwatching*, as we say in Nicaragua (same story as *Math Zero at the U—looks* like I do my best work under pressure).

In my third year at the university, I fell in love with the one who stole my heart: Leyda Fonseca. That ended my plans of becoming a priest. Some friends told me not to marry her; so we only had a civil ceremony. Had it been otherwise, God's plans for me wouldn't be what they are today. At the UCA, those who wished could attend Mass celebrated by Father Santiago de Anitua, who also taught us Philosophy in his lecture course. During that relationship, César Ricardo was born.

Earlier, in my fifth year of high school, I'd fallen for a very beautiful girl with a strong, sensual voice: Odilie Castro. My brother Javier teased me endlessly about it. No—no children from that relationship. Many years later, already in the United States, she asked if I'd written my book—apparently I'd once told her I would. I said no, that it was still pending. Her father had businesses and owned passenger buses running between Masaya and Managua. During my first semester at the university I sometimes rode one of those buses because it left very early; he gave the order that I shouldn't be charged the fare. (On that bus there was a striking, elegant woman studying Law at the UCA; I liked her a lot, but one day I found out she was married. Lord have mercy—married women are off-limits.) The free-bus blessing ended when I broke up with the owner's daughter.

Seeing me downcast, my mother said—cutting to the chase:

"Son, remember: the student's girlfriend is not the doctor's wife."

I still managed to ride the bus through the following semester. (And don't forget, my Uncle Armando often picked me up.)

The UCA's buildings had been destroyed by the Managua earthquake of December 23, 1972. We studied in newly built, earthquake-resistant facilities. In 1974, when I enrolled, the rector was Father Arturo Dibar, a Jesuit from Uruguay, who replaced the founder Father León Pallais, after tensions with students during those politically turbulent times. The vice-rector was Father Juan Bautista Arrien from Spain, a standout on the UCA soccer team. Later, Father Arrien became my second rector, and by the time I graduated, the rector was Dr. Indalecio Rodríguez, the first layperson to hold the post (formerly the dean of Agriculture).

Those were years of extreme political violence, and many students, intellectuals, politicians, and respected professionals—opposed to the Somoza regime—lost their lives. Even so, I managed to graduate.

Between first and fifth year of high school a lot happened to me… and, oh yes, from kindergarten through sixth grade, too. One thing at a time.

Chapter 6.5
Early School Years
— In Love, Maybe?

During my grade school years, after classes I'd head straight to the field to play ball—baseball, of course. I don't know if I was much of a hitter, but I do remember being a good catcher, always crouched behind home plate, glove ready.

Back then, I became friends with José "Chepito" Echegoyen and Alejandro Moncada, son of the director of the Nicaraguan Red Cross. I had many good friends in childhood, but none like my lifelong brother of the heart: Dr. Gerardo Sánchez Vega.

A brilliant physician, incredibly intelligent—he was the top student in Masaya, and later, one of the best in all of Nicaragua. A good son and grandson, too: grandson of Don Adán Sánchez Cerda, founder of the Masaya Red Cross, and son of Carlos Adán Sánchez, a well-known teacher and former baseball player for the San Fernando team. I can't forget Gerardo's grandmother, Doña María Jesús Bermúdez de Sánchez, owner of the store La Giralda.

Gerardo is a devoted husband and father; all his children are professionals. When we were kids, we'd ride his bike around Masaya at night, visiting girls and trying to charm them—just to see who'd get lucky. Gerardo fell for a beautiful girl named Janett Ortega, who later became a Doctor of Pharmacy. And in time... he married her!

Girlfriends? Oh, I had a few—well, more than a few, all of them very pretty... but that's a story for later..

A Friendship for Life

My everlasting friendship with Gerardo began like this: we were in second grade at Conchita Alegría School, one block from his house and three from mine. One day, I forgot both my notebook and my pencil (my irresponsibility was already showing). The teacher began dictating a lesson, and I froze—I didn't know what to do.

Seeing my panic, Gerardo quickly pulled out an extra notebook and a pencil, smiled, and said:

"Here, use this to write."

The desks were the old-fashioned kind—two students to a bench, with space underneath for storing notebooks. We sat side by side. From that day on, we became inseparable.

I'm the godfather of his eldest daughter, Dr. Karla Sánchez Ortega. Nearly twenty years after I'd left Nicaragua, Gerardo, Janett, and Karla—by then married with daughters—came to visit me in the U.S. I told Karla the story of how I met her dad. She smiled and said,

"That's such a beautiful friendship you two have."

And it's true. To this day, every May 19, I call to wish my goddaughter a happy birthday.

Javiera—Was She My First Love?

At Conchita Alegría, I was in second and third grade. Across from the school lived a cheerful, popular girl named Javiera Valle, who I really liked—and she knew it.

One morning, while I was waiting for school to open with Gerardo, Javiera walked up to me and asked:

"Julito, do you like me?"
"I don't know about you…" I replied.
"I like you."
"Well then, I like you too."

I never knew if we were actually boyfriend and girlfriend. Her brother Chema became a good friend of mine too—I loved watching him ride his motorcycle. Sadly, Javiera died in a car accident in 1976, at just twenty years old. The whole city of Masaya went into mourning. The crash was with another young man from the city, Jorge Bolaños, son of Nicaragua's former president, Engineer Enrique Bolaños.

Other Childhood Friends

From a young age, I also became friends with Tito Lagos, now a successful journalist and entrepreneur living in Los Angeles, California—I owe him a visit. I still keep in touch with Jorge Correa Montiel, now a Doctor of Law.

At Conchita Alegría School, I sometimes hid to avoid going to class… but I'll save that for Part II – The Bad.

In sixth grade, my teacher Argentina Ríos—a very beautiful woman, by the way (she married Máximo Montenegro Escorcia, brother of one of my girlfriends, Maritza Rodríguez Escorcia)—chose me and my friend Rodolfo Miranda Escobar (Pepe) to compete for the award of *Best Elementary Student.*

Gerardo, who attended another school, didn't take part. I didn't win first place—too playful for that—but Gerardo did. He was recognized as the best elementary student in all of Nicaragua.

Well deserved..

Chapter 6.6
Starting High School

My first year of high school was at the prestigious Salesian School of Masaya. I made many friends there. When my Uncle Eduardo came to visit my mother, the two of them would pick me up at the end of the school day.

That same year, I studied alongside someone who would later become a great friend—and a witness at my civil wedding to Patricia—Dr. Óscar Cuadra Ocón (may he rest in peace). In 1986, while I was in Cuba advising on the production of sulfited sugar, I returned home to the sad news of his passing. I immediately wrote him a poem and gave it to Celia, his widow.

Óscar teased me endlessly at the Salesiano… and, of course, I teased him back. Among my mischievous moments, I remember bothering another student who would later become a renowned poet and writer—Julio Valle-Castillo. One day, he got his revenge: as he passed by my classroom window (I sat near it), he grabbed a fistful of my hair and yanked so hard that my scalp hurt for a week.

Óscar, who sat behind me, liked to jab me in the back—or worse, in the rear—with a pencil. Who would have thought that later we'd become such close friends, along with Gerardo and another dear one: Filiberto "Filín" Vega (Q.E.P.D.), a relative of Gerardo. That same year, I also shared classes with Alejandro Velázquez (Q.E.P.D.), another cherished friend from my youth. Years later, in Florida, my wife and I cared for him during his final days of illness. Our friend José Rodolfo Miranda (Pepe) even traveled from Texas to help out.

We used to play soccer and baseball in Gerardo's enormous backyard. When the ball went over into Dr. Cornelio Hueck's yard, we'd politely ask permission to get it back. Gerardo's property also backed up to the schoolhouse of Don Manuel Maldonado, whom I'll mention later. His grandfather, Don Adán, raised rabbits—and, thanks to our mischief, more than one ended up injured!

Óscar Cuadra was the owner of our soccer team, Las Águilas del Ixtac—a name suggested by Filín, who was dating Guadalupe, the sister of Maritza. We were fourteen years old then, right at the age when we traded baseball for soccer. We became the best youth soccer team in Nicaragua, winning the Junior Major League championship two years in a row.

From the Salesiano to the INMA

I transferred to the Instituto Nacional de Masaya (INMA) in my second year of high school and graduated from there in 1973. My mother decided to move us because my brother Javier had failed his first year at the Salesiano. She told us:

"I can't keep paying tuition at a private school if you're not taking advantage of the opportunity."

And that was that.

The INMA wasn't a bad school—in fact, it was one of the best public high schools in the country, directed by Dr. Carlos Vega Bolaños, a man highly respected nationwide, and staffed with outstanding teachers. Among them were:

- Dr. Enrique Peña Hernández, author of the textbooks Spanish Language and Literature; lawyer, writer, member of the Royal Spanish Academy, and later professor of Law at the UCA.

PROGRAMA

1. Entrada de Bachilleres

2. Himno Nacional

3. Palabras de Ofrecimiento por el Br. Rafael Urbina seguidas alumno de la Promoción

4. Entrega de Diplomas al homenajeado por la Sra. Margoth Dariagan

5. Agradecimiento: Prof. Manuel Rocha M.

6. Intermedio Musical

7. Discursos Especiales
   — Club Rotario
   — Instituto Nacional de Masaya
   — Instituciones en General

8. Palabras alusivas a la Promoción

   Lic. Omar Lucio Reyes
   DIRECTOR DEL INSTITUTO

9. Entrega de Diplomas y Anillos

10. Acta Premio "B" Por Br. Oral

11. Clausura del acto

    Lic. Ricardo Reyes Lira

12. Poema

13. Salida de Bachilleres

INSTITUTO NACIONAL DE MASAYA

"Rafael Cabezas Núñez"

BODAS DE PLATA

XXV

PROMOCION
DE
BACHILLERES

PROFESOR

Manuel Rocha Marenco

1948 — 1973

El Personal Docente, la Dirección del Centro y la Vigésima Quinta

"PROMOCION DE BACHILLERES"

Prof. Manuel Rocha Marenco

Invita a Ud. para el acto de Graduación, el 8 de Diciembre a las 5 p.m., en el Salón de actos del Inst. Nac. de Masaya;

y para el "TEDEUM" en acción de gracia en la Parroquia de nuestra Señora de la Asunción, a las 4 p. m. del mismo día.

Diciembre, de 1973.   Masaya, Nic.

BACHILLERES

Martínez Putoy Dora
Medina Flores Martín Rafael
Mejía Cuadra Pedro José
Mercado Garay Vesta María
Mercado Parrales William
Miranda Aguilar Mayra del Socorro
Miranda Chavarría José Eligio
Miranda Díaz Antenor Edgar
Miranda Escobar José Rodolfo
Molina Morales Ruth del Carmen
Monjarrés Paladino Javier
Montealegre Calero José Antonio
Morales Avilés Bosco Alejandro
Morales de Núñez Elena
Morán Orozco Mercedes Isabel
Murillo Pérez Leonel Antonio
Murillo Pérez Marvin José
Navarro Espinoza Fernando José
Noguera Espinoza Martín José
Noguera Flores Aníbal José
Noguera Flores Daniel Antonio
Núñez Hernández Walter
Namendy Caldera Rosa Angélica
Oppenheimer Monteagro María Lorena

Calero Moya Manuel Ernesto
Cárdenas Alvarado Miguel Ramiro
Castillo Caldera Iván Antonio
Castillo Caldera Pablo
Castillo Caldera Marvin
Castillo Caldera Ramón Mauricio
Castillo González Ana Cecilia
Centeno Gómez Sonia Auxiliadora
Cerrato Vásquez Mariela del Carmen
Collado González Darlyn
Córdoba Dávila Adán Antonio
Córdoba Úbeda Portilla Rafael
Cortez Mayorga Ramón Enrique
Cruz Espinoza María Nela
Cruz Márquez Olga Dolores
Cruz Luna Emma Dora
Cruz Luna Manuel Antonio
Dávila Altamirano Alberto
Dávila José Hermes Alberto
Díaz González Jorge Luis
Díaz González Raúl de Jesús
Duarte López Enrique
Duarte Membreño Miguel Ángel
Espinoza Brenes Irlanda

Fernández Rocha Eduardo Alfonso
Flores Luna Raúl
Fonseca Bermúdez Fátima Ileana
Gaitán Herrera Miriam Dalila
Gómez Morales Mariana
Gómez Morales María Dolores
González Melender Luis de la Concepción
González Mora Roberto Enrique
González Pérez Félix Segundo
González Pitters Xiomara
González Ruiz Francis de la Cruz
González Solórzano Manuel de Jesús
Guadamuz Duarte Francisca Antonia
Guerrero Potosme Manuel Antonio
Guerrero Potosme María Asunción
Gutiérrez Martínez Ruth del Carmen
Guzmán Brenes Justo
Jiménez Ramírez María Verónica
José Flores Carlos Iván
Lacayo Sánchez Henry Hugo
Leiva Gómez Vilma del Socorro
Lovo Pérez José Orlando
López García Judith Luz
Maitena Silva Oralia Rosana

BACHILLERES

Ordeñana Calero Mayra del Socorro
Ortega Castillo Claudia Ofelia
Ortega Escobar Manuel Alberto
Ortega Valdez Lucy Jeannette
Padilla Meléndez Mercedes del Socorro
Paniagua Gaitán Margarita Auxiliadora
Paniagua Sánchez Rudy Antonio
Pastora Guerrero Martha Lidia
Prado Parrano Roberto José
Pérez Flores Naúl Antonio
Pérez Marín Luis Manuel
Pérez Silva Rita Lorena
Ramírez España Silvio René
Ramírez Obregón Mario Javier
Rivera Marín Sidar Enrique
Rocha Marenco Hercilia
Rodríguez Manzanares Oscar Enrique
Rodríguez Álvarez Gloria del Carmen
Ruiz Cruz Leslia Verónica
Salgado Hernández Mercedes del Carmen
Sánchez Álvarez Susana de los Ángeles

Sánchez Calvo Odel Enrique
Sánchez Díaz Silvio José
Sánchez Rojas Lesbia María
Sandoval Mecharra Rosa Argentina
Sandoval Torraba J. Alejandro
Siles Ortega María Isabel
Sevilla Sevilla María Nelly
Somarriba Leyton Alan
Soza Blanco Francisco José
Tapia Roa Wiseo
Téllez Reyes Guillermo
Téllez Álvarez Adriana del Carmen
Téllez Guillén Gladys Danaris
Téllez Martínez Róger Alfonso
Téllez Mora Roberto Jose
Trejos Gómez Lesbia de Socorro
Trejos Maldonado Enell Jerovano
Trejos Maldonado Melba
Trejos Vega Edgard Enrique
Vanegas Chávez Miguel Ángel
Vargas Solís Eduardo
Vega Gutiérrez Maritza del Socorro
Vega Jiménez Carlos José
Velásquez Palacios Heberto Zacarías
Vidaurre Pérez Rosa María
Villarreal Pérez Róger Sebastián

Abauza Sánchez Yamil
Abea Vargas Bertha Julia
Acevedo Sánchez Miriam
Alvarado Sánchez Niosska Angélica
Alvarado Benavides Vicente Rafael
Álvarez Pérez Noel
Ambota Saazo Lidia del Socorro
Aragón Caldera Rosa Antonia
Araúz Molina Teresa del Carmen
Arias Flores Julio
Arias Flores Sergio Francisco
Arias Flores Silvio Antonio
Artola Guerrero Porfirio
Baldizón Rocha Marisol de los Ángeles
Ballesteros Tukeu José Ismael
Barrios Jirón Celina Mata
Bendaña Alegría Mario José
Bonnes Beza Rubia del Socorro
Brenes Soza Berta del Socorro
Bustos Ortega María Mauricia
Caldera Boza Rigoberto José
Cabrera Dávila José Benjamín
Caldera Fuentes Jaime
Caldera Koder Roxmel

- Teacher William and Dr. Antonio Espinoza, both outstanding teachers.
- Eng. Roberto Bermúdez, who once served as secretary to the poet Rubén Darío.
- Lic. Manuel Rocha Marenco, to whom we dedicated our high school graduation.
- Lic. Violeta Berríos, who taught us Literature in our final year.

With Professor Berríos I had a memorable little episode. One day, right in the middle of class, she asked me a question. I paused for a moment, thinking, and said:

"Ideay, wait a second, I'm thinking."

She replied,

"Julio, don't say ideay to me."

And I insisted,

"Ideay, but what do you want me to say?"

That was the end of the class!

Years later, when I was already in college, she became my professor again in a master lecture on Spanish. When we met again, we both remembered that scene and laughed heartily about it.

The Context of the Times

We graduated from high school in 1973, just one year after the massive earthquake that destroyed Managua. The refugees who came to Masaya were affectionately called "los terremoteados"—literally, "the earthquaked ones."

1972 was also the year of the Amateur Baseball World Series, held in Nicaragua from November 15 to December 5. It coincided, as I mentioned earlier, with the December 23rd earthquake. That World Series featured legendary international players, including Roberto Clemente, center fielder for the Pittsburgh Pirates, who had just hit his 3,000th career hit that same season. He came as the manager for Puerto Rico's team.

Shortly afterward, Clemente tragically died in a plane crash while carrying relief supplies to Nicaragua. In his honor, the baseball stadium in Masaya now bears his name, and the Nicaraguan national team wore his number—21—on their uniforms, the same he wore for the Pirates.

Remember I told you about the daughter of the bus company owner who used to let me ride to Managua for free? Her parents also owned Joyería Elizabeth, a prestigious jewelry store. That store won the contract to engrave the names on the gold plaques for the World Series trophies. They asked if I wanted to make a little money helping out. I learned to use a small engraving machine—similar to a typewriter but with a granite tip—to carve the letters. There were many trophies, and yes, I made some nice extra cash. What a great time!

Many of the "terremoteados" went on to study and graduate from the INMA. One of them was my college classmate, Engineer Pánfilo Rafael Córdoba Úbeda, who went on to achieve one of the highest academic averages in the history of the UCA.

Chapter 6.7
University Years

At the UCA, I made many great friends. One of them, Ángel Ortega, a Spaniard, once introduced me to a beautiful young woman named Rosa Pasos. When she told me her name, I replied playfully:

"You're Rosa, and everything else is just bud."

("Chote" in Nicaragua means a rose that hasn't bloomed yet.)

I never heard from Ángel again—he left the country during Nicaragua's political turmoil. As for Rosa, in time she joined the Sandinista Front (FSLN). During the war against Somoza—after the assassination of Dr. Pedro Joaquín Chamorro—I ran into her in Masaya. I greeted her, but I don't think she remembered me. Maybe someone had told her sweeter compliments than mine.

And that was the end of that story—the parrot died there, as we say back home. Later, I learned she had held an important position in the Sandinista government.

Campus Life

During my fourth year of Engineering, I worked at the university as a lab assistant in Chemistry and Instrumental Analysis, and also as a report proofreader. (That's when I met the student Bárcenas, whom I mentioned earlier.)

Around that time, I bought my first car: a two-door Fiat 127. Oh, if that little car could talk—it would have stories to tell! A classmate, Miguel Barrios, had a similar one, a four-door Seat. Years later, after graduation, I ran into him again—he was then the administrator of the San Antonio Sugar Mill, representing the FSLN, which had taken over the mill previously owned by the Pellas family.

At the UCA, I made many good friends and classmates: Javier Will Baca, Alberto Lacayo, Javier Vallecillo, Lorna, Camacho, and others to whom I even ended up giving classes—Barney Chamorro, Milton Gómez, Orlando Gómez (no relation between them), Camacho, Ocón, and several more whose names I can't quite recall..

Ajedrez y respeto académico

Chess and Academic Respect

One afternoon I walked into a group of classmates playing chess: I remember Antonio Barrios (an excellent student and the only one who later became a priest), Carlos Velázquez, Salomón Calvo (the UCA champion), someone with the last name Fonseca, and another named Franco.

I asked,

"You guys playing chess?"
"Yeah," one of them replied. "Want to play?"
"Sure," I said. "But it's been a while since I've played."
"Doesn't matter," said Carlos. "When this match ends—and Salomón wins, as usual—you'll play him next."

And that's what happened. I sat across from Salomón, the university champion. After about an hour and a half of an intense match... checkmate!

From that moment on, I earned the respect of the top Engineering students. How about that?

I also had many good friends among the girls at the UCA: Verónica Wheelock Horviller, one with the last name Noguera, another Ramírez, and several more.

Chess at Home

Even before that, the Moncada-Paladino clan and our friends used to hold chess tournaments at my house. We were passionate about this "sport of the mind." Our circle included Jimmy Moreno, David Calvo (Salomón's brother), my brother-in-law Carlos Jarquín, the Mormon missionaries, and even once Henry Lacayo, the chess champion of Masaya.

I managed to last forty minutes against him—a personal record I still brag about!

My brother Javier, on the other hand, became INMA's champion in the beginner's category.

Chapter 6.8
Adventures

Among the beautiful adventures of my youth, the first was being a Boy Scout—part of the worldwide organization founded in England by Lord Baden-Powell. During those years, I traveled to almost every Scout camp in Nicaragua. The only thing I missed was attending a Jamboree, the world gathering of Scouts hosted by a different country each time.

The mottos "Always Prepared" and "Once a Scout, Always a Scout" have stayed with me for life.

Around that time, Hernaldo Zúñiga and I competed to see who would be the pitcher for our neighborhood baseball team. I won, but I told the coach to pick Hernaldo too—and thank God, he did. We both made the team. To be honest, though, I can't remember if that team ever actually played a single game! (Haha.).

Volcanoes and Odysseys

Together with friends and my brother Javier, we climbed Masaya Volcano three times. First, we would hike up the slopes of black volcanic rock to reach the Santiago Crater, always fuming and alive. Then we'd continue to the Masaya Crater, a little higher up and so close to the first it felt like a twin volcano. It was dangerous—one wrong step could send you tumbling down into Santiago's smoking mouth.

Inside the Masaya crater there was vegetation; we even saw deer grazing below. We would circle around the rim, facing toward

Laguna de Masaya, and from there descend through thick forest. The descent was dim—the trees were so tall they blocked out the sunlight. The jungle was alive with snakes, wild pigs, monkeys, and deer. Thankfully, we never came across any panthers or ocelots… though I'm sure they saw us.

We ran downhill carefully, as dripping water made the soil slippery. At the base, we'd cross a dry field of hardened lava until we reached the far end of the lagoon near Nindirí, where we'd dive into the cool water to refresh ourselves after the exhausting hike.

The climb back was the hardest part: a steep 200-meter cliff known as Las Escaleras de Nindirí—"the Nindirí Stairs." Thick tree trunks served as steps, and the rocks had carved footholds, with roots and branches as makeshift handrails. It was true extreme sport.

Local women used those same stairs daily, carrying baskets of laundry on their heads to wash in the lagoon below, then climbing all the way back up. Real-life acrobats! When we crossed paths with them, we had to flatten ourselves against the narrow trail to make room—and avoid falling to our deaths.

The entire journey lasted about six hours: a bus ride to Piedra Quemada (about 8 km from Masaya), two hours on foot to the Santiago crater, another hour to Masaya crater, two hours descending, one hour across the plain, a swim in the lagoon, and another hour climbing back up. An odyssey indeed. By God's grace, none of us ever got hurt on any of our three trips.

Coyotepe and Hernaldo

We also hiked to Fort Coyotepe, a fortress hill facing Masaya along the Pan-American Highway. The site, rich in national history, had been donated by President Luis Somoza Debayle to the Nicaraguan Scout movement, which turned it into a museum of arms. Before that, it was a military post and the battleground of General Benjamín Zeledón.

One day, climbing the hill with the Zúñiga brothers, Rigo Cabezas, and the Calvo Arrieta brothers, one of the boys slipped and almost fell into the ravine. Miraculously, Hernaldo Zúñiga grabbed him by the collar and saved his life.

Years later, Hernaldo moved to Chile, became a famous singer and songwriter, and went on to win Silver Seagulls at the Viña del Mar Festival.

When we were young, we also used to serenade our parents on Father's Day in Nicaragua. I didn't sing or play an instrument—I just tagged along. (That's still on my list of things to learn.)

Years later, around 1987, I ran into Hernaldo at the Hotel Intercontinental in Managua. I asked him for an autograph and a dedication for my sister-in-law Nelly Amalia (Patricia's sister). He kindly obliged, with his usual humility.

Vacations and Summer Loves

I spent several Holy Week vacations in San Juan del Sur, a beautiful town with a spectacular beach, and also in San Jorge, Rivas, on the shores of Lake Nicaragua (Cocibolca), facing the majestic twin volcanoes Concepción and Maderas on Ometepe Island.

There, I fell for a young woman—I think her name was Marta—and later heard through the band Los Signos del Zodiaco that she had asked about me at a party in Rivas.

Another favorite spot was the Laguna de Apoyo, with its slightly salty water. We stayed at the summer house of my friend Alberto Robleto, camping in tents. I remember on December 22, while driving in his Land Rover Jeep, we listened to José Feliciano's Feliz Navidad. None of us could have imagined that at dawn the next day, December 23, Managua would be struck by the great earthquake.

We were a big group at the lagoon: my brother Javier, Jorge Correa (a dear friend with whom I used to drive around Masaya in his father's car), the Brenes brothers—Antonio and Alberto, nicknamed "Los Calines"—Iván Castillo, and several others.

On Holy Thursday nights, big parties were held at the famous Pelayo Bar, where the "Queen of the Lagoon" was crowned. She would later compete for the title at the Balmoral Hotel in San Juan del Sur.

At the lagoon, I had a platonic crush on Patricia Huembes, niece of Lila Huembes (my sister Elizabeth's godmother). I never confessed my feelings. At a party, I asked her to dance, but so did another guy—at the exact same time. We both tugged gently at her hand until I stepped back, seeing how nervous he got.

Years later, I ran into her at the UCA, where she was studying Law alongside my sister-in-law Tere Velázquez Brenes. During the war—or perhaps before—she got married and left Nicaragua.

Childhood Memories

As a child, my parents often took us to the beaches of Montelimar, Masachapa, and Pochomil, all along the Pacific coast of Managua. We also visited the Great Lake of Nicaragua (Cocibolca)—a place I'll never forget.

Chapter 6.9
My Birth

And here we go! I was born on November 9, 1955, under the sign of Scorpio—intense, magnetic, loyal, and passionate.

That year, while I came into the world in Masaya, the planet itself was spinning toward a new era. The world was caught between wars, inventions, and collective dreams. And right in the middle of those historic shifts, there I was—a tiny soul, unaware that one day I would become a witness to many of those transformations.

The decade of my birth was one of great change and turning points in history:

- The overthrow of Juan Domingo Perón in Argentina, marking yet another swing in Latin America's political pendulum.

- The creation of the Warsaw Pact, the Soviet response to NATO at the height of the Cold War.

- The arrest of Rosa Parks in the United States, whose simple act of courage helped ignite the Civil Rights Movement.

- The opening of Disneyland in California and The Mickey Mouse Club, awakening the imagination of children everywhere.

- A major medical breakthrough: the polio vaccine began saving lives and restoring hope to families around the world.

- The Le Mans disaster (1955)—a tragic racing accident that shocked the globe, with 83 lives lost and over 100 injured.

- Walt Disney released Lady and the Tramp, destined to become an all-time animated classic.

- Technology began making its way into homes: the first Tappan microwave oven and Zenith Flash-Matic wireless remote control, created by Eugene Polley, changed daily life forever.

- And that same year, the first McDonald's restaurant opened in Des Plaines, Illinois, without the faintest idea of the global empire it would one day become.

So it was—in the midst of political upheavals, technological leaps, children's laughter in new theme parks, and the first steps into a modern way of life—that my story began. The world was getting ready for great change… and I, from my small corner of Masaya, was getting ready too.

Chapter 6.10
In Love

From a very young age, I've been a hopeless romantic.

At my first school, a little kindergarten called Los Párvulos—located in the home of poet and writer Manuel "Melico" Maldonado and his sister Aurora—I had my first "love": my teacher, Sonia Guillén. She was young, beautiful, and elegant. I was just a little boy, but already completely smitten. Years later, I learned she married a doctor.

In second grade, I fell for Javiera, whom I've already mentioned earlier. In third grade, for a girl whose name I can't recall, but I still remember her flowered dresses and sweet little face.

In fourth grade, I attended a school in the San Juan neighborhood, near the San Antonio Hospital in Masaya. There, I became friends with Ronald and Horacio Guillén—better known as "Lacho"—as well as Eligio Miranda, Humberto and Leopoldo Díaz, and Julio Flores and his sister Jilma, with whom I nearly became boyfriend and girlfriend.

Curiously, there were three different boys named Julio Flores in that neighborhood—none related! Around that time, I used to ride around the streets of Masaya on Gerardo's bicycle, feeling like the king of the world.

In fifth and sixth grade, to keep from boring the reader (though you may not believe it), I was also in love—twice, actually. This time with Rosibel Maltéz, daughter of Professor Julio Maltéz and sister of Celina, my brother Miguel's friend; and with Jazmín Valle, daughter of a transportation businessman who ran the Masaya–Managua route (apparently I had a thing for bus families, as I mentioned in my university days). Jazmín's brother, "Chele" Valle, was my classmate in fifth grade and became a talented baseball player, just like Francisco "Chico" Pavón Pineda, my classmate in fourth year of high school—both of them members of Nicaragua's National Baseball Team.

Back then, Gerardo and I used to visit the girls—sometimes just to walk past their houses, smile, and wave if they happened to be outside. Eventually, of course, they started dating other boys. But by then, I was already off chasing new dreams. I never stayed too long tangled in any single *"romance."*

Teenage Years and High School Days (1969–1973)

Then came high school—and the famous quinceañera parties, which I couldn't possibly miss. The girls were everywhere—"seven to one," as we used to say, like the córdoba-to-dollar exchange rate back then. And after the "terremoteadas" (the earthquake refugees from Managua), there were even more!

Maybe it was that flirty, festive spirit that caused me to fail my second year at the INMA… but that's a story for Lo Malo (The Bad).

It was also during that time that I started playing soccer seriously. I was a solid goalkeeper, a strong defender, and even scored two goals as a striker against the team Patria from Granada.

Our team, Las Águilas del Ixtac, was made up of Óscar Cuadra, Filiberto Vega, Gerardo Sánchez, Andrés Sánchez, Julio Moncada, Antonio and Javier Rodríguez Escorcia, Jesús González ("Chico Lepra"), Segundo Flores, Moya, and others.

That's when my most famous nickname was born: *"CocaCola."*

It was Omar Blandón who came up with it, saying my body looked like the bottle—small head, wide torso, and skinny legs. From that moment on, all over Masaya I stopped being Julio—I was *CocaCola*. The nickname spread so far that even at the Sugar Directorate, everyone knew me by that name.

High School Highlights

The fourth and fifth years of high school were wonderful. In fourth, I liked a girl named Irlanda Espinosa, who had "that something" that made her special. My friend Miguel Duarte used to tease her constantly, until one day we tied him to one of the INMA columns and the teachers had to order us to untie him!

That same year, we cried when Dr. Carlos Vega Bolaños, our beloved principal, retired. That's when I learned that INMA's full name was *Instituto Nacional Manuel Coronel Matus*, honoring a distinguished son of Masaya.

We also went on school trips to places like *El Salto de Estanzuela* (Estelí), Jinotega, Matagalpa, Chinandega, and even Costa Rica and Panama, thanks to a brand-new bus Dr. Vega Bolaños had secured for the school.

Around that time, Catholic charismatic groups were blossoming. People would point at us and say, "He's one of the charismatics," as we rode to Managua on Fénix buses, singing loudly:

"Alabaré, alabaré, alabaré a mi Señor…"

In fifth year, we organized an internal baseball tournament among all grades. One of the most unforgettable moments was when a tiny base runner collided with the burly catcher Miguel Cárdenas, knocking him flat and scoring the winning run! The caricatures—our version of today's memes—immortalized the moment: a baby chick toppling a giant rooster.

We also celebrated the election of the INMA Queen and the "Ugly King."

That year, our class won both titles: Xiomara González ("Xiomara I") as Queen and Silvio España Ramírez ("Silvino I") as King. The coronation party was unforgettable: parades, floats, a full-blown street carnival in Masaya, and a dance at INMA's grand halls, with music by Los Hermanos Cortez and Los Ramblers.

It was a glorious era, one I still treasure with deep affection

Reflection

Looking back on all those early loves, the quinceañeras, the serenades, soccer games, and school pranks, I realize now that none of it was just youthful folly or fleeting crushes. Every smile, every illusion, every heartbreak taught me to value life's beauty, the meaning of true friendship, and the importance of feeling deeply.

Being "in love" was never a flaw—it was a gift from God, one that taught me to see the good in people, to live with joy and passion. That restless, playful heart that once fluttered for a glance or a kind word is the same heart that later recognized—and forever cherished—the true love of my life: Patricia.

Today, I understand that those first loves were like rehearsals—training chapters for the great story that would become my life.

And if there's one thing I'm certain of, it's that being such an incurable romantic in my youth made me a man who feels deeply, gives fully, and loves his family without reservation.

Chapter 6.11
Athlete

In fifth year, I already mentioned my girlfriends—but what I hadn't told in detail was how I began to stand out as a soccer player in the infantil mayor (junior major) division. At that stage, I was a very good goalkeeper—it wasn't easy to score on me.

However, during a match between Ixtac and Salesiano, played on the field of the Salesian School, Armando Ramírez—a striker from that school, Guatemalan-born but of Nicaraguan descent and grandson of Don Miguel Ramírez—scored two goals on me! I was so upset that I decided to stop being a goalkeeper altogether. I walked off the field crying in frustration and switched positions to right-back defender. It was the first time we ever lost a match... and to make things worse, it was a friendly!

In the league tournaments played on the field of Barrio La Reforma—on land kindly lent by Don Andrés Vega—our team became champion two seasons in a row. Competing teams came from different neighborhoods: La Reforma, San Juan, El Calvario, El Oratorio (an annex of the Salesian School, directed by Father Marcolla), and of course, Ixtac.

As years passed, we moved up to the Youth League, which later opened to all age categories. Matches were played again at the Salesian field. Teams included San Juan, El Calvario, El Oratorio, Omar Blandón and Julio Flores's team, and our eternal rival, El Rocha, sponsored by General Rocha and his daughters—among them the popular Amada Rocha, who later married my friend Edgard Velázquez.

That team featured greats like Rómulo Acevedo, Iván Castillo, "El Chele" Lara (whom I later met again in California), Hugo "Bazuca" Huete (I saw him in Miami in 2007), and Manuel "Catarrito" Cuadra, all former UCA players.

Later, I joined El Porta, a team sponsored by my university friend Eduardo Porta Córdoba, also an engineer (he in industrial, I in chemical-industrial). We became league champions. The team included Eduardo Porta, Jorge Brenes, Carlos Brenes, Mario Rosales (RIP), Mario Bolaños, Augusto Pallavicini, one of Eduardo's cousins with the last name Córdoba, and me, among others. A truly great team!

First Division and the Rise of Deportivo Masaya

From there, I made the leap to Nicaragua's First Division, joining Deportivo Masaya (formerly Deportivo Chávez), sponsored by

El Deportivo Masaya, sorprendente equipo.

Dr. Arnoldo Chávez and his wife Doña Matty. The team earned promotion undefeated.

I witnessed that final match myself—against ISA (Ingenio San Antonio) at Cranshaw Stadium in Managua. What a team that was! It featured stars like *"El Pipil"* from El Salvador, Oldemar Moncada from Costa Rica, Omar Blandón, Bergman Masís (our eternal captain), Ramón "Capeto" Castillo Caldera, *"Pillina"* Ramírez, *"Pildorita"* González, "Palomo" Flores, and Ronald and Miguel Bolaños, among others.

In 2018, the Arnoldo and Matty Chávez Soccer Complex was inaugurated in honor of their contributions to sports in Masaya.

I still remember the day clearly: I was in Production Control class at the UCA when Engineer Ronald Bolaños came to get me—to sign with Deportivo Masaya. I played with that team for about six years, as well as in several matches for the UCA itself, as I mentioned earlier.

We even participated in the Cuadrangular, a tournament for the top four teams in the national rankings. Deportivo Masaya won the National Cup in 1983, the very year I retired. By then, I was already Director of Industrial Operations at Ingenio Javier Guerra.

Later, in 1984 and 1986, Deportivo Masaya became national champion, but I was no longer on the field—I had fully devoted myself to my professional career.

The Goalkeeper Returns

In a memorable match against Diriangén, played on the field of Colegio La Salle in Diriamba, our goalkeeper Ronald Bolaños was expelled for rough play. I, who was playing right-back, took over as goalkeeper.

It was one of my most unforgettable performances—I prevented what could have been a heavy defeat with several diving saves. We still lost, but the score had already been sealed before I put on the gloves. After the match, Ronald said:

"Moncada is the revelation between the posts—he'll be my replacement."

But I stuck to defense, my true position.

Many of my teammates later shone in other clubs or even became national team players, like Julio Flores. I played my final match in the Masaya Open League around 1982–1983, at the age of 30… just before winning over Patricia's heart.

Reflection

Sports, to me, were far more than a pastime or youthful competition.

They were discipline, effort, friendship, and life lessons.

On the field, I learned to win with humility and lose with dignity, to respect my teammates and opponents, and to work as part of a team to achieve goals greater than my own.

Every goal conceded, every clean play, every championship and defeat taught me something essential: that life is also a team sport, that today's sweat becomes tomorrow's satisfaction, and that perseverance turns a dreaming boy into a man of character.

Though I hung up my cleats at 30, soccer never left me. It lives on in my memories, in my friendships, and in the lessons that still guide me today.

Sports gave me the strength to face life with courage—and unknowingly, prepared me for the greater challenges ahead: my career, my family, and my destiny.

Chapter 6.12
Here and There: My Mentor, Dr. Jaime Downing

The time came for my graduation exam and the presentation of my thesis before Dr. Jaime Downing, who immediately offered me an internship. There was no party or graduation ceremony in 1978 due to the country's turmoil; the UCA authorities decided to suspend it. I first received my diploma from the Universidad Centroamericana, and months later, my Engineering degree from the UNAN (Universidad Nacional Autónoma de Nicaragua), in March and May 1979, respectively, just before the final insurrection led by the FSLN.

At that time, university diplomas were signed by the President of the Republic, who then was Anastasio Somoza Debayle. I didn't want my degree to bear his signature, so I kept it unsigned, aware that his fall was imminent and afraid of losing it. Once Somoza was overthrown and the country stabilized, I submitted it for the official signatures. It was no longer signed by Somoza but by the Secretary General (an illegible signature) and the Rector of the UNAN, Mariano Fiallos Oyanguren, in August 1980. Later, I thought perhaps it would have been better to keep Somoza's original signature, but it was too late… and as we say, "what might have been doesn't exist."

In late 1978 and early 1979, Dr. Downing recommended me to Pan Bimbo, which was looking for a chemical engineer to manage production. I worked there for about three months, but I resigned for three reasons: first, the owner, Luis Pallais Jr., was the son of Dr. Luis Pallais Debayle and cousin of Somoza, which put me in a politically sensitive position. Second, I was picked up in a car with armed escorts, and I feared that the Sandinistas might mistake me for someone else and kill me. And third, I realized I didn't want to be a "bread engineer."

Still, I understood why a chemist was needed in a bakery: controlling humidity, temperature, dew point, and the famous Gaussian curve are essential in the baking process. It was interesting, but not my path.

From there, Dr. Downing recommended me to Engineer Jesús Campos, Regional Manager of Adhesives at MERINSA–Kativo Nicaragua, a subsidiary of Fuller (U.S.A.). I took charge of the adhesives division, replacing Engineer Roberto Mongalo, who had been promoted to Production Manager of Pinturas Kativo, replacing Engineer Roberto Fajardo, who in turn moved to Pinturas SUR.

It was there that the 1979 insurrection caught me. Many companies were burned or looted, and Kativo was no exception. They offered to transfer me to Costa Rica, but I chose to stay in Nicaragua. At that time, my girlfriend Leyda had moved to Venezuela. Meanwhile, I started dating a beautiful young woman who worked at a Kativo store in Managua. However, I made a mistake: I disappeared without saying goodbye, supposedly to avoid hurting her—but I know it was worse. When Leyda returned, we resumed our relationship, and from that union, César Ricardo was born. Eventually, we separated in 1982, as there was no future together.

When Kativo was confiscated, my mentor appeared once again: Dr. Downing gave me a job at POLYCASA as assistant to Engineer Alvaro Martínez, Production Manager, who later became Deputy General Manager. The previous assistant had died during the war. Shortly after, the owners of POLYCASA fled the country, including

Donald Spencer, and the company passed into the hands of the Sandinista government. What happened afterward, I already told in The Good Part, beginning with ATCHEMCO and my great friend, Engineer José Luis Howay.

Reflection

If there was a key figure in my professional life, it was Dr. Jaime Downing. He was more than a boss or teacher—he was a mentor who opened doors, offered his hand in difficult moments, and believed in my abilities even before I did. His trust led me to industries, challenges, and responsibilities that shaped my career.

Thanks to him, I learned that knowledge isn't only shared in the classroom but also through guidance, support, and the willingness to give others a chance. Every step I took after university carried, in one way or another, the mark of his influence. And for that, his name deserves to be written in these memories with respect and gratitude.

Chapter 6.13
Professional Relationships

Throughout my professional career, in every company I worked for, I had the blessing of being surrounded by intelligent and capable professionals. Leading them all, without question, was my eternal mentor, Dr. Jaime Downing Urtecho (R.I.P.), founder of the Chemical Engineering program at UCA.

I'll never forget one of his famous lines, when someone tried to bypass his authority:

"Look, I invented you—and I can un-invent you too."

Among other great colleagues and teachers, I remember with deep gratitude Eng. José Luis Howay (R.I.P.), Eng. Esteban Duque Estrada, Eng. Roberto Fajardo, Eng. Jesús Campos (R.I.P.), Lic. Fernando Cajina (R.I.P.), Eng. Edgard Vargas Guzmán (R.I.P.), Eng. David Morice Gallegos (R.I.P.), Eng. Wilfrido Mierish, Eng. Antonio Vargas, and Eng. Eduardo Holman Chamorro.

Experience in Cuba

Between 1986 and 1990, I served as chief advisor for sulfited white sugar production in the Republic of Cuba. The results were so successful that I was asked to travel twice a year to follow up on the work done at the Ingenio Amistad con los Pueblos and six other Cuban sugar mills.

When the MINAZ (Cuba's Ministry of Sugar) and the DIA (Nicaragua's Sugar Industry Directorate) invited me to work in Cuba, my response was:

"One swallow doesn't make a summer. I'll go—but I'm taking selected workers from each sugar mill in Nicaragua, because this is a team effort."

And that's exactly what I did. I selected two operators from each stage of the sugar process and took Patricia, my newlywed wife, along as my personal secretary.

In Cuba, I was directly assisted by Vice Premier of MINAZ, Raúl Trujillo Tejeda, and at the mill, by General Director Eduardo Fraga. The results were so remarkable that upon returning to Nicaragua, Edgard Vargas (National Director of the Sugar Industry) and Eduardo Holman (Deputy Minister of MIDINRA) appointed me Industrial Coordinator of Nicaragua's Sugar Mills, a position I held until 1990.

Later, I invited the directors of Cuba's sulfited sugar mills and their chief technicians to Nicaragua, so they could see our process firsthand. I personally accompanied them through every sugar mill in the country, along with Olman Rodríguez, who was part of the team hosting the Cuban delegation.

Innovations in the Sugar Industry

From there, I moved on to METAZÚCAR, the metal-mechanical branch of the sugar industry, under the leadership of Eng. Wilfrido Mierish. During that period:

- I dismantled a massive sugar dryer with giant cylinders from Ingenio San Antonio and reinstalled it at Ingenio Victoria de Julio, setting up the full industrial equipment to produce sulfited white sugar—a product they had never been able to make before. The results were outstanding.

- At Ingenio Benjamín Zeledón (formerly Dolores), I installed a double-seed system with excellent outcomes.
- At Ingenio Germán Pomares (Monterosa, El Viejo, Chinandega), I implemented the double purge system for seed C.
- In Honduras, I achieved crystallization of molasses without changing the process—producing a quality of sulfited sugar never before reached—and improved the juice clarifier design.
- At Monterosa (Nicaragua), I redesigned the molasses clarifier, which had not worked properly under its original design.

Each project was a technical challenge and a professional triumph that filled me with pride.

Hard Times

Of course, not everything was smooth sailing. During some of my hardest times—usually when changing jobs and going months without employment—I experienced the humbling moment of returning a brand-new car to the dealership and walking again, riding the bus to Managua with a briefcase full of dreams.

In those difficult seasons, I always found kind-hearted friends who lifted my spirit:

- Lic. Gonzalo Duarte, whom I met at UCA, and his wife Olga, whom he affectionately called Olguita, living in Colonial *Los Robles*.
- Eng. Mario Gómez, owner of a steel factory in Tipitapa and a commercial building in Managua.

- And, of course, my lifelong mentor, Dr. Jaime Downing, who even visited my distillery at my farm *Gracias a Dios*.

Those tough times strengthened my character. Like the Phoenix, I always rose again from my own ashes. And through it all, the presence of the Lord God never left me.

Chapter 6.14
Thanks Be to God: El Trapiche

During 1992 and 1993, I produced bulk aguardiente (raw rum) and sold it throughout the southern departments of Nicaragua—Masaya, Carazo, Granada, and Rivas. Bulk meant selling it by the gallon, in 5-gallon containers, or even by the liter—the smallest unit of measure.

In 1993, before I moved to Honduras (in 1995), I bought a sugarcane farm with a small mill *(trapiche)* called "La Vida es Nada"—"Life Is Nothing." I changed its name to *"Gracias a Dios"* (Thanks Be to God). It was located in the sugar-mill region of Carazo, between Nandaime and Jinotepe, right along the Pan-American Highway.

There, I designed, built, installed, and started up a distillery capable of producing 96° G.L. alcohol (96% purity) at a rate of 800 liters per day. Everything started from the sugarcane mill. I also built a small steam boiler to power the distillation column, which allowed me to extract alcohol from the fermented molasses obtained from the crushed cane. That potable alcohol was sold as aguardiente, reducing the alcohol content to 35–40° G.L., as required by law.

I designed the distillery to work by gravity, needing only two propulsion pumps—one of them a dual-direction gasoline pump.

I remember once inviting Gerardo and his family to the farm to take a dip in a huge cement tank that looked just like a swimming pool.

Support and Setbacks

One day I went to Ingenio San Antonio in Chichigalpa, Chinandega, to visit Edgard Vargas, who was then the General Manager, looking for material support to finish the distillery. Edgard authorized some supplies, but the superintendent, Eng. Wilfrido Mierish, refused to release them.

Eng. Guillermo Ramírez, who had been my advisor at Ingenio Javier Guerra, also showed great interest in the project and even visited me to see how it was progressing.

At one point, I even built a couple of small evaporator pans (tachitos) to produce sugar, though I never installed them—I decided to finish the distillery system first.

The Economic Blow

Production eventually came to a halt when Licorera Nacional, the producer of the famous Flor de Caña rum, drastically lowered the price of its bulk aguardiente. That blow made my operation unsustainable.

In August 1995, Edgard Vargas called me and offered a job at Ingenio La Grecia in Marcovia, Choluteca, Honduras. I accepted and worked there for a year until Edgard resigned as manager. My results were excellent—we achieved a quality of sulfited white sugar never before produced at that mill.

The Move to Monterosa

In 1996, Edgard came to my property along with Architect Ramiro Lacayo Deshon. They offered to buy my distillery, on the condition that I dismantle it and reinstall it at Ingenio Monterosa (formerly Germán Pomares), hiring me as Distillery Manager.

I immediately agreed. I kept the original design but improved it, even building a 60-HP boiler from discarded materials found at the mill.

- During that period, I received three very special visits:
- Eng. David Morice, factory manager at Ingenio San Antonio;
- Dr. Jaime Downing, my lifelong mentor, who was then a technical consultant;

Eng. José Luis Howay, who had been living in the United States since 1982.

Later, Ramiro and his cousin Dr. Raúl Lacayo Solórzano, owners of Ingenio Monterosa, asked me to also take charge of sugar production as Head of Manufacturing, since they hadn't been able to produce sulfited white sugar. I ended up with two salaries, managing both operations—and once again, the results were excellent.

However, Monterosa was later sold to Grupo Pantaleón of Guatemala, led by Julio Herrera, whom I met when he visited the mill. The distillery was not included in the sale, so I dismantled it and brought it back to my Gracias a Dios farm, storing it safely under a roof.

The Mill for Rent

I later rented the trapiche to Mr. Ramón Conrado. I would grind my cane in the mornings to make atados de dulce (brown-sugar blocks), and he used the mill in the afternoons and evenings. That partnership worked smoothly through 1997 and 1998.

Unshakable Faith

Today, sadly, unscrupulous people have tried to take over the farm, destroying the distillery and the entire trapiche.

Faith Beyond the Good, the Bad and the Ugly

But I know that the earth belongs to the Lord, and everything in it. What seems like loss to man is only a pause to God. I firmly believe that everything taken from me in this world, God will return in multiplied form—in peace, in family, in blessings, or in new opportunities.

That's why, every time I think of my farm Gracias a Dios, I don't see it as destroyed—I see it as a seed still planted in fertile soil. A seed that, in God's timing, will bear fruit once more.

Chapter 6.15
Grateful Friends

In July of 1999, my friend Olman Rodríguez Sequeira came to visit me from the United States. He was working at the Osceola Sugar Mill in Florida. He asked how I was doing, and I explained that I had left the sugar mills to start my own company for producing alcohol and, later, sugar—but that I hadn't been able to continue because of the strong monopoly of Flor de Caña.

With his usual generosity, Olman said to me,

"Come with me—let's give it a try at the mill where I work. Maybe you can start there."

I told him yes, but added honestly that I didn't have money for the plane ticket. Without hesitation, he loaned me the money.

Arrival in the United States

On July 28, 1999, I left Nicaragua on an American Airlines flight bound for Miami. I arrived with one large suitcase—filled more with engineering books than clothes. My total cash was thirty-five cents, but my real wealth was my faith in God, my experience, and my determination to chase new opportunities at forty-four years of age.

At the Miami airport, I was met by my brother-in-law Carlos Jarquín Rojas, husband of my sister Elizabeth, who, by coincidence, had arrived in the U.S. just one day before. He took me to Homestead, where Elizabeth and Carlos were staying with friends—Jacobo and

Ofelia, a Nicaraguan couple who had settled in Florida. That's where I spent my first night in America.

The next day, I learned that one of my cousins, Socorro "Coco" Paladino—sister of my cousin Armando Paladino, founder and drummer of the band Los Rockets—lived in Sweetwater, much closer to the airport. I contacted her, and the following day Carlos drove me to her home. I spent only one night there, but it was long enough to talk by phone with my uncle Armando, who was also living in the U.S. We reminisced about the old days when he used to give me rides to the UCA on his way to work at Nabisco Cristal in Managua. That was the last time we spoke, as he passed away not long afterward.

The Road to Pahokee

Early the next morning, I went back to the Miami airport to meet up with Olman and Manuel Rodríguez, brothers I had known since our days at the Ingenio Javier Guerra in Nandaime.

Olman was a tachero—the top position in a sugar mill, back when sugar crystallization depended on a craftsman's hands and instincts, not machines. Manuel, his brother, had started as an assistant, but over time, with my recommendation and the support of Don Carlos Parrales (R.I.P.), our maintenance chief and later my personal advisor, he was promoted to tachero as well. From then on, the two brothers worked side by side and earned a reputation as outstanding craftsmen in their field.

Together, we headed to Pahokee, a small town about two hours from Miami, on the southwestern shore of Lake Okeechobee—Florida's great lake, though still much smaller than our own Great Lake of Nicaragua. The sugarcane region extended to nearby towns like Belle Glade, South Bay, and Clewiston.

The First Visit to the Mill

The following day, they took me to the Osceola Sugar Mill, where they worked. They introduced me to the Factory Director, but his answer was brief and blunt:

"I don't have any work available… not until November."

I left with my head down and my heart heavy. I needed to send money to my family as soon as possible. I felt the ground shift under my feet—but I also understood that I hadn't come all this way to give up.

Reflection

That was the beginning of my journey in the United States. There was no gold or silver waiting for me—only faithful friends, gratitude in my heart, and a deep conviction that God would open the right doors.

If I learned anything from that time, it's that friends placed on our path are instruments of God—and that a loan given in trust, a bed offered for a night, or a phone call made at just the right moment can mark the beginning of a whole new life.

Chapter 6.16
First Job in the United States

Back in Pahokee, my friends often stopped at a gas station to buy a few beers. One day, the attendant working at the pump got into an argument with the owner, Mr. Emilio Pérez, and quit on the spot. Seeing an opportunity, Olman, Manuel, and I spoke with Emilio and asked him to give me a chance. Since he urgently needed a new gas attendant, he hired me right away.

The pay was $300 a week, working from 4:00 a.m. to 8:00 p.m. I could also have sodas and food from the store in exchange for helping carry the meat for the restaurant next door. I accepted without hesitation. That's how my journey began—in August 1999.

At that time, I was living with Olman and his family in an apartment near the gas station. Every dawn, a pack of stray dogs would show up looking for food. I used to share some scraps with them, especially with a black dog who seemed to be their leader. I treated him kindly, and—almost unbelievably—he became my protector. Every night at 8 p.m., he would walk beside me from the gas station to the apartment, and at sunrise, he'd be waiting at the door to escort me back. Every single day.

One day, overwhelmed by emotion, I broke down in tears and said to myself:

"Here stands Engineer Julio Moncada, once Coordinator of Sugar Mills in Nicaragua—successful in every company he ever worked for—now pumping gas like an attendant..."

News of this reached Nicaragua and spread quickly. Yet I felt peace in my heart, because I was able to send money to my family and had already repaid the $330 that Olman had lent me for the ticket.

From Gas Attendant to Administrator

After twenty-one days at the gas station, I spoke with Emilio and told him I was an engineer. Olman and Manuel confirmed it, and Emilio decided to give me a new opportunity: he offered me a position at his office in Belle Glade, starting in September 1999.

So I went from being a gas attendant to becoming administrator of all his properties, which included:

- 63 rental houses
- A transport operation with 12 trucks (4 owned and 8 subcontracted)
- A mechanic workshop

At first, Olman lent me his car to commute.

When I learned that my sister Elizabeth and her husband Carlos were unemployed in Miami, I spoke with Emilio to ask if he could hire them as well. He agreed, and they came by train from Miami. I picked them up at the West Palm Beach station, and Emilio even provided them a house free of charge, right across from the gas station. I moved in with them, returned Olman's car, and began traveling daily from Pahokee to Belle Glade in one of the company's trucks—leaving every morning at 4:00 a.m.

Stories and Scares

One early morning, as I got off a truck in front of the office, two Dobermans guarding a nearby car dealership charged straight at me. I shouted with all my strength:

"STOP!"

Incredibly, both dogs froze in place and backed off. I was trembling with fear.

Another time, as I was stepping down from a truck driven by a Nicaraguan named Luis, my foot slipped from the step and I fell headfirst. Luis ran toward me, terrified, thinking I had broken my neck. What a fright! Thank God, I only had minor bruises.

Trust and the First Christmas

Through hard work and responsibility, I earned Emilio's trust. By December 1999, he handed me $1,500 so I could return to Nicaragua, bring my family back, and continue working for his company, EMISAR (named after *Emilio and Sara*, his wife).

Before that trip, in November 1999, Hurricane Irene swept through Pahokee, toppling trees and damaging countless homes. The house where I lived was hit hard—the glass windows were completely destroyed. It was a painful reminder of how fragile life can be… yet also of how strong we can become when faith and hope hold us up.

Chapter 6.17: Trip to Nicaragua and Return to the U.S. with My Family

I left the United States on December 5, 1999, through Panama, on my way back to Nicaragua. Patricia's birthday was on the 7th, so I arrived just in time to celebrate with her. The rest of the money for my return to the U.S.—$800—was given to me by my brother Javier, who had been living there for several years, working as a dentist. He was married to Dolores Sansoni, and together they had four wonderful children: Eduardo Javier, Laura Isabel, and the twins Andrews and Matthew.

We returned to the United States as a family on December 27, 1999, the Feast of the Holy Family. We flew into Miami and then made our way to Pahokee. It was nighttime, and no one was there to pick us up. I hired a taxi from the airport that initially charged $220, but I managed to negotiate it down to $180. There were seven of us—Patricia and I, along with our five children. The trip took two hours. We arrived at Olman's house at about three in the morning. Everyone was asleep during the ride; Patricia carried little Gonzalo, almost two years old, on her lap.

Days later, Patricia told me that as she looked out the window at the dark, empty highway, she silently wondered:

"Where is Moncada taking us?"

That night, the temperature had dropped to about 40°F (4°C).

When we finally arrived, Olman's wife, Verónica, a kind and devout woman, received us warmly at 2:30 a.m. and let us in. When Olman got home from work around 7:30 a.m., he started counting the children and said, laughing:

"Wait, we're missing one—I only counted four, and there are five!"

He hadn't seen Gonzalo, who was still fast asleep in Patricia's arms. We laughed about that mix-up for years afterward.

A Humble Beginning

The next day, a lady from Masaya—whom I vaguely remembered from my soccer days at the Salesiano school—took us to the house where we would live, a property owned by Emilio. The house had been vacant for five months, with no water or electricity.

We managed to find two mattresses: Gonzalo slept inside a suitcase stuffed with clothes to keep warm; three of the children shared one mattress, and Julio Jr. slept in a long duffel bag, covered with clothes. Patricia and I shared the other mattress. We were happy—because we were together.

(Today, all those children are grown—married, educated, and professionals.)

During those first days, we would eat and bathe at a nearby Kentucky Fried Chicken, while I had already resumed work with Emilio.

On the third day, I noticed Patricia sitting quietly on the only metal chair in the house, looking deep in thought.

I asked her,

"Patricia, what's wrong? Are you sad? Are you feeling sick?"

She replied softly,

"No, Julio, I'm fine."

Later, she confessed that she had been thinking to herself:

"What am I doing now? Do I go back or do I stay? If Jesus, the Son of God, was born in a manger, what more could I ask for, being no one?"

She also remembered the words of a Neocatechumenal priest who once told her:

"A marriage must not live apart—either all together in the U.S., or all together in Nicaragua. If your husband must live up in a tree, that's where the whole family belongs—united, not divided."

Providence Arrives

That same day, someone knocked on the door—it was Mr. José Ramos, whom I had met at the gas station. When he learned about our situation and faith, he brought us a dining table, stove, two beds, and bedding. A lady named Wendy gave us a refrigerator and microwave, Sara (Emilio's wife) brought living room furniture, and I bought a used TV, desk, and bookshelf. Slowly, the house began to look like a home again.

We even had a scare or two—three snakes appeared in the house: one near me, one near my daughters, and one near Patricia. All three met the same fate.

Before leaving Nicaragua, we had sold many of our belongings and given others away. But God, in His infinite kindness, returned everything—and more than we needed.

Do you believe in God? There's your answer.

Closing a Chapter

When I finished working with Emilio, on November 1, 2000, I handed over everything in perfect order: payments for 63 rental houses, 64 freight trucks hauling mulch, sticks, and bagasse for the Okeelanta power plant, and the four EMISAR trucks transporting sugarcane. Emilio was well respected because he paid well and on time, which made his company highly sought after by truckers from Miami and Fort Myers.

However, Emilio didn't want me to move to Okeelanta. In fact, he even notified the HR manager there that I didn't have legal papers. The truth was that, when we entered the U.S., we were granted a six-month tourist stay, and not knowing the immigration laws, we missed the chance to apply under the 245(i) law, valid until April 2000, which allowed residency petitions between siblings. Patricia had her citizen sister Braxis, and I had my brother Javier, but we never pursued it.

A Door Opens Through Faith

The letter of recommendation from Father John to Engineer Ricardo Lima, manager of Okeelanta, eventually bore fruit. One Sunday, during Mass at St. Mary's, Engineer Lima announced a job opening. No one approached him, so I ran home to grab my résumé and the letter.

Patricia said,

"Run, I'll keep him here until you get back."

While I was gone, she chatted with Mrs. Lima, who was Honduran and shared her love for sewing and tailoring—Patricia's passion.

When I handed my papers to Engineer Lima, he said:

"Don't worry, just give me Father John's letter. You already have the job. Ask for Mr. Israel Báez at Okeelanta."

Later, Mr. Báez told me I'd need to regularize my immigration papers before starting as Production Supervisor. Concerned, I went back to Father John, who gave me a check to help with expenses. Glancing at it, I thought it said $250, but when I opened it at home, it read $2,500!

God bless Father John!

A member of the church community referred me to Richard, a Haitian man who could help with the paperwork. He assured me my work permit was legitimate since my Social Security number matched the one I had applied for back in 1992. We even went together to retrieve it from a Social Security office in North Miami. There was no doubt it was valid. The whole process cost $2,500, which also covered Social Security numbers for Patricia, Julio Jr., and Gonzalo—the three girls already had theirs.

Chapter 6.18: Church Work and Travels

Throughout all the years I worked at Okeelanta, we were tireless collaborators in God's Kingdom through St. Mary's Church. We helped Father John in any way we could—Patricia served as secretary for catechesis, and I supported various parish activities. On Valentine's Day, I even took part as a "judge" in mock weddings, handing out symbolic marriage certificates—what a fun and joyful celebration that was!

We celebrated every Marian devotion, especially the Immaculate Conception, patroness of both Nicaragua and the United States. Though there were only a few Nicaraguans in Pahokee, we made our presence known with joy and enthusiasm—singing the traditional songs to the Virgin and loudly proclaiming our beloved refrain:

—*"Who brings so much joy?" —"The Conception of Mary!"*

Among our fellow Nicaraguans in Pahokee were Ivania Larios and her family, a lady named Jeanette, Auxilio Miranda, and several others. We invited the entire community—mostly Mexican—to share in our traditions, just as we joined in theirs.

Patricia led celebrations for the Sacred Heart of Jesus, St. Jude Thaddeus, and the Rosary in its different Marian devotions. With the help of Ivania, who served as president of the parish council, we also organized events for Father John Mericantante's birthday, his priestly anniversaries, and other parish celebrations.

We taught faith classes for adults, and fifteen minutes before the 11 a.m. Sunday Mass, we shared parish announcements and news with the congregation. Father John gave us his blessing to start a radio program on Radio Lobo in Belle Glade, which we called Family Catholic Portal: *With Jesus Christ at the Center of Our Lives.*

The program was sponsored for ten months by Mr. José "Pepe" Fanjul Jr.; another month was covered by the production supervisors at Okeelanta, and four months we funded ourselves. We aired every Sunday from 7 to 8 a.m., and the show was very well received by the local Catholic community. Sadly, the station later shut down due to lack of funds.

During the eighteen years I worked at the Okeelanta sugar refinery, I lived with deep happiness and gratitude. I had a stable job in my profession, a good salary, growing experience, and my children were advancing in their studies until they finally graduated from college.

In September 2016, Patricia, Bryan, and I traveled to California, spending three days in Las Vegas along the way. We then rented a car and drove to Maricopa, Arizona, where we visited my brother Javier for two days before continuing to California to see Patricia's sister, Nonga.

On May 30, 2018, I retired at the age of sixty-two and a half. We moved from Pahokee to West Palm Beach. Since then, we've made several road trips: three times to California, twice to Washington, D.C., and New York, once to Chicago and Niagara Falls, another time to Massachusetts to visit Harvard, Cambridge, and MIT, and one more to Atlanta. We've also traveled extensively throughout Florida.

Chapter 6.19
Patricia, the Lovely Girl

I wanted to save this story for last—on purpose. After all, the last shall be first.

When I first arrived at the Javier Guerra Sugar Mill, I walked into the Engineering Office. On the left side sat a group of technicians, and right in front of me I saw a beautiful young woman, sitting at her desk, focused on her work. I was struck instantly—love at first sight—and a thought raced through my mind: "She's the one." Was that the Holy Spirit whispering to me?

They later took me to another office, where the Consejo de Zafra (Harvest Council) met, and introduced me as the new Factory Superintendent, replacing Mr. Egnio Arauz, who had been reassigned to Jesús María Mill, which only produced molasses. Three days after I arrived, the young woman disappeared and never came back. Curious and disappointed, I asked my secretary, Asunción Sánchez, who she was and why she had left without saying anything.

Asunción explained that the young woman had only been completing her production hours to qualify for high school graduation. Her name, she said, was Ana Patricia Ramírez León, and she came from one of the wealthiest families in Nandaime. I did some asking around and found out she was the granddaughter of Don Alfonso León Sam, a Chinese immigrant, and Doña Leonor Abaunza Miranda—and the daughter of Doña Nelly León.

A few months passed, and Asunción became pregnant. I needed a temporary secretary during her maternity leave, so Human Resources sent me two candidates. Neither could handle the workload or the pace of the Superintendent's Office. Before leaving, I asked Asunción to find the lovely girl to replace her. I even got HR and some of the factory workers involved to help persuade her. They spoke with her mother, Doña Nelly, who finally convinced her, saying she had nothing to lose by trying. And that's how it happened. I was thrilled—my "top" was spinning right where I wanted it.

I courted her for almost a year, even though she already had a boyfriend. One day I told her, "I'm going to make you forget that boyfriend—you'll marry me instead." Time proved me right.

I fell madly in love with her and stole many wonderful kisses—something that today would probably be called harassment, but back then, it was a different time. Patricia had been crowned Queen of the Patron Saint Festivities of Nandaime, in honor of Saint Anne, grandmother of our Lord Jesus. For the parade, she had to ride a horse. I showed up on my Honda 750 motorcycle after having a few drinks at a friend's house. When I saw her, stunning in her cowgirl outfit, mounted on her horse, I jumped up and climbed behind her. Nervous, she feared the horse might take off and begged me to get down. I told her I would—if she accepted me as her boyfriend. She was caught off guard, so I stepped down and left.

That night, at the gala, I went looking for her to dance, but I saw her with her boyfriend—and she kissed him right in front of me. I lowered my head and muttered to myself, "To hell with it."

The next day, the mill's executives and I traveled to Cuba as a reward for having been recognized as the best sugar mill in Nicaragua. We had an amazing two-week trip. On our way back, at the urging of José, our General Manager, I bought a beautiful necklace for Patricia. When I returned to the mill, I placed it around her neck with a big kiss. By then, she had broken up with her boyfriend. Bit by bit, she forgot about him, and I went to meet my future mother-in-law. I was honest with her, telling her I had a son from a previous relationship—and that sincerity won her over. She welcomed me into her home. My father-in-law, on the other hand, couldn't stand me—he was "locked in" against me and made no effort to hide it.

Once, during a secret visit, he came home armed with an AK-47, ready to shoot me. Thankfully, I had already left. Another time, he came out swinging a machete, causing a huge commotion that my mother-in-law managed to contain by locking the doors. He even shouted insults at me in the house of Don Carlos Parrales, my maintenance advisor at the mill. Eventually, I took my father to meet him. When he learned that I was the nephew of Dr. Eduardo Paladino, whom he knew personally, his anger began to fade. Quite an odyssey, wasn't it? But it was worth every moment.

Over time, Patricia has said that, at first, she couldn't stand me—to which I always reply, "You must've really disliked me, since you gave me six children!" People always laugh when they hear that.

On January 23, 1986, we were married in a civil ceremony, and two days later, on January 25, in the Church of Saint Anne in Nandaime, my father-in-law proudly walked the lovely girl down the aisle to give her away. God granted me the victory and the deepest desire I'd carried from the first day I saw her: that Patricia, my lovely girl, would become my wife.

When I was imprisoned before our wedding, I thought my father-in-law might intercede for me—but it was in vain. He was the cousin of writer and politician Dr. Sergio Ramírez Mercado, who at that time was Vice President of Nicaragua in the government of Commander Daniel Ortega Saavedra, both members of the Sandinista National Liberation Front (FSLN).

To be continued in: The Bad, Chapter 11.

Chapter 6.20
My Father and Mother In-Laws

The relationship between my my father and mother in law and me was, to put it mildly, a disaster—I already mentioned that in The Good, Chapter 6.19. Would I have done the same in his place? Please, go back to that chapter and judge for yourself.

In truth, my father and mother in law was quite a character. Everyone called him El Hermanazo—"The Big Brother." Over time, he softened a bit, though never completely toward me. He loved telling jokes—hundreds of them—but repeated them so often that I used to tell him he should just number them to make things easier. He prided himself on being related to the renowned writer Sergio Ramírez Mercado—and indeed, he was.

My in-laws once lived in Venezuela, where they raised their first four children: Nelly Amalia (may she rest in peace), Gonzalo José (may he rest in peace), María Leonor—whom we all call Nonga, my "big sister"—and Ricardo Antonio. Later came Braxis Auxiliadora, Ana Patricia, and Javier. In Venezuela, my father and mother in law did very well—he was twice awarded national recognition as the top life insurance salesman in the country. Later, he founded a pest-control company that also prospered.

Anecdotes About My In-Laws

Once, during his days traveling all over Venezuela selling insurance, my father and mother in law used to go on the road with a colleague named Mendoza. My mother-in-law, suspicious of his escapades, decided to follow him. The two men checked into a hotel in Caracas (though they lived in Maracaibo), and my mother-in-law booked the room right next door, disguised with a wig, dark sunglasses, different clothes, and strong perfume so he wouldn't recognize her.

There was a small hole in the wall between the rooms. To catch their attention, she turned up the music and began to dance. Curious, they took turns peeking through the hole. She slipped a little note through it, asking for a cigarette. Delighted, they said they'd bring it to her door, but she insisted they pass it through the hole. My father and mother in law, amused, brought his mouth close to the hole, trying to kiss the fingers of this mysterious woman. Then she spoke—and he froze. "That's my wife!" he shouted to Mendoza. Seconds later, she stormed into the room, and chaos broke loose.

Back in Nicaragua, my mother-in-law opened a store called Kikatex, which later became La Familia, complete with a sewing workshop. My father and mother in law, for his part, opened a butcher shop and another pest-control business, both of which thrived. He traveled all over the country fumigating homes—and also selling the clothes my mother-in-law's shop made. But he was quite the ladies' man, and she caught him more than once.

In Estelí, for instance, she discovered he was having an affair with a young woman he'd told he was single and planning to marry her. My mother-in-law, ever clever, disguised herself as a gold jewelry saleswoman and approached the unsuspecting girl, saying she had brought engagement rings "sent by Mr. Gonzalo Ramírez" for her to choose from. When the girl confirmed the story—boom! Another huge scandal erupted.

Remembering My Mother-in-Law

My mother-in-law treated me like a son. She passed away in 2005. Patricia couldn't be with her because we were in the middle of our immigration process in the United States. Still, she carried the peace of knowing she had been a devoted daughter—as Doña Nelly herself used to say. During her final illness, she was cared for by another daughter, our dear "Nonga."

She lived long enough to share life with all my children except Bryan, whom she never got to meet. She used to ask my daughter Braxis, then only eight years old, to follow her grandfather and report back on who he talked to and what he did. That was my mother-in-law—sharp, watchful, and full of heart.

The legacy she left is profound: she raised her daughters to be loving wives and mothers, and her sons to become strong, responsible fathers.

The Death of My Father and Mother in Law

My father and mother in law died in 2009, just a few months after my own father passed away, of a heart attack. The circumstances were somewhat strange. Only a month earlier, he had been visiting us in Pahokee during one of his trips to the United States. Oddly enough, he left behind a piece of farmland as his inheritance—but he never signed the proper document. Instead, they only placed his thumbprint on it, even though at the time he was living with another woman.

Before his death, he had been examined by my lifelong friend, Dr. Gerardo Sánchez. My brothers- and sisters-in-law remember him fondly, and to be fair, he was a good man—just not to me. I understand why; we had once gotten into a heated fight while both of us were drunk.

Here's a curious story: a photograph surfaced showing my father and mother in law and my father when they were young. One stood at the far right and the other at the far left, surrounded by their fellow workers from the Ferrocarril del Pacífico de Nicaragua (Pacific Railroad of Nicaragua). The amazing part is that, although they appeared in the same picture, they never actually met! My father-in-law had kept that photo tucked away in his old trunk of memories.

Chapter 6.21
Friends in My Golden Years

As you've read in the previous chapters, I've always been surrounded by friends—since childhood, through my teenage years, young adulthood, university, and all throughout my professional life. Friends from every walk of life and from every community where I've lived and worked. And through it all, Gerardo has always been my best friend.

As time goes by, we grow older, meet new people, and life itself begins to change—and so do we. Some changes are for the better, others… not so much. Through all those shifts, it's essential to hold tightly to the moral values instilled in us by our parents and mentors, so we don't fall into temptation or stray from the right path.

About ten years before my retirement, I met a family with whom I slowly built a bond so strong it has lasted to this day. They aren't strangers to the León family, Patricia's relatives, since they share family ties. I'm speaking of the couple William and Irene Doña-Morice and their children—Bernardo, María Teresa, and Irene Auxiliadora—descendants of honorable families from the department of Rivas, Nicaragua. Irene is the sister of Dolores, widow of Ernesto León, who were Patricia's uncle and aunt.

With them, we've shared moments of joy and sorrow as if we were one single family. For that reason, they deserve special mention: true, loyal friends in one's later years are not easy to find.

Gerardo and his family, together with this wonderful family that God placed in my life, are my two treasures of friendship. As Scripture says, "Finding a friend is like finding a needle in a haystack." And the Lord, in His mercy, has placed these two "needles" along my path to remind me how precious the gift of true friendship really is..

PART II: THE BAD

Chapter 1
Nightmares

Oh boy... here comes the bad. Remember what I said in the introduction to this story. I'll begin by going back to my childhood. Nothing I write in this part is worth anyone repeating—it belongs to the past.

A child, in his innocence—after the age of five and following baptism—can already sense what is good and what is evil... though only as a perception, nothing more.

When I was about three or four years old, every night I would tell my mother that a man was trying to take me away—as if to kidnap me or steal me from her. Thank God, my mother took me seriously. She brought me to Monsignor Vela Matamoros, the parish priest of the Immaculate Conception Church in Masaya, who was a good friend of hers.

The priest prayed over me, gave me his blessing, and sprinkled me with holy water. That was the cure—after that, I never had that feeling again. Was it the Evil One trying to torment me, trying to pull me to his side? Maybe... I've always felt I have a powerful personality and a certain magnetism that draws people—and perhaps things—toward me.

Chapter 2:
Hiding Out

When I was in second grade, there were times—well, more than a few—when instead of going to school, I'd sneak into an empty lot near our house. I'd spend the whole day there playing marbles and making up the homework I was supposed to have done for the next day.

Getting into that lot wasn't easy. It didn't have a fence—just a dirt mound about ten feet high, which made it hard to climb. But I always found a way. Once inside, it became my own little world of imagination and escape.

One fine day, while I was playing, I heard a whistle—the same whistle my mom used to call us home! To my surprise, there she was, standing right on top of that dirt mound, staring straight at me. She only asked,

—*"What are you doing here?"*

Then came her verdict:

—*"Starting tomorrow, you won't be skipping school ever again."*

How did she discover my big secret? How did she know exactly where I was? She never told me. I think someone must've seen me go in early and, noticing I didn't come out until around the time school ended, told her. Yes, that must've been it.

I thank God that in those days there weren't the dangers children face now—no predators lurking around. Skipping school? Never again! Honestly, it hurt more to be caught than to be scolded.

I'd done my first grade at a private school run by Doña Olivia Urbina. She was very strict and carried a big ruler she used for discipline. That approach worked well on my brothers—but not on me. Even as a child, I didn't like being corrected or told what to do; I only accepted it from my mom. I guess you could say I was a bit spoiled. I just hope you've learned how to correct that little non-virtue better than I did.

Chapter 3:
The Papaturro Tree

Do you remember when I told you about the papaturro tree? It was a giant—its branches wide and generous, its glossy leaves casting a cool shade where the air felt softer and even the birdsong seemed to change its tone. Its fruit, sweet and juicy, hung high above us, teasing us children from the heights as if daring us to come and get it.

One day, determined to reach those tempting fruits, I climbed up and found myself perched on a branch about twelve feet off the ground. The adrenaline rushed through me—I felt like a circus performer. Then, fate played a trick on me: I slipped.

In that split second, between fear and instinct, I did the only thing my body told me to do—I threw myself toward another branch, like a monkey swinging through the jungle. And miraculously, I caught it with both hands! I slid down to the ground in what, to me, felt like an acrobatic feat worthy of Cirque du Soleil.

My daring stunt quickly became the latest craze. All my friends started copying it: we'd climb up, leap for the same branch, and swing down like amateur trapeze artists, landing in a storm of laughter and excitement. For us, it was pure fun; today, I see it for what it was—a bit of sheer madness.

So let me say this seriously: no young person should ever try such a stunt! The danger was very real, even if we, in our innocence, couldn't see it then.

And that's how the papaturro tree became part of my childhood legend—a stage for adventures, laughter, and near-misses that, thank

God, never ended in tragedy. I was only in fourth grade at the time, but I already thought I was a world-class tightrope walker.

Chapter 4: Intolerant and Disrespectful

At the Salesian School, when I was in my first year of high school, something happened during recess—our mid-morning break around 10 a.m. to unwind between classes—that I'm still ashamed of. I grabbed a basketball and threw it toward a group of students who were reading the school's bulletin board. Of course, it was a terrible thing to do.

The Prefect Father, who was also the school's Director, saw me and immediately signaled for me to come over. He pulled out a long metal chain—the kind he used to keep his keys—and gave me a lash across the back. I managed to dodge most of the blow, but it still caught me, leaving a scratch that stung badly. Ouch! If that hit had landed fully, I don't even want to imagine…

I moved on to my second year of high school, as I've already mentioned in The Good. But I didn't make it to the third year—I had to repeat the second. My behavior was still irresponsible, and I was especially disrespectful to my English teacher, Mrs. Dina Bermúdez. I bothered her all year long until, one day, while she was writing on the board, I threw an eraser at her. She turned around just in time and dodged it—the eraser hit the board instead. When she scolded me, I had the nerve to tell her that I was "going to date one of her daughters."

That was the last straw. She took me straight to the Principal's Office, where they called my mother. Mrs. Dina, who actually knew my mom, explained what had happened and told her that, because of my behavior, she wouldn't pass me for the class. And that's how I ended up repeating the second year—just because of English.

The following year, English was taught in the afternoons by Professor Pablo Castillo (father of Iván and Pablo). To keep myself busy, I enrolled as an auditor in the third-year Spanish Literature class, taught in the mornings by Dr. Enrique Peña Hernández. None of this is something I'm proud of—quite the opposite. I share it as a warning: please, don't follow my example!

The most curious part of that period came after Holy Week, which I spent at the Huehuete beach resort in Carazo. I had gone with my sister Elizabeth, who'd been invited by the family of her boyfriend (and later husband), Carlos Jarquín. We were swimming in a tide pool surrounded by big sea rocks when suddenly a small octopus latched onto her leg. You can imagine the panic! We all tried to peel off the tentacles that clung tightly with their suction cups. Finally, we managed to free her and tossed the creature back into the ocean.

When classes resumed, Dr. Peña Hernández asked his students to write a short essay about their Holy Week experiences. Even though I was only auditing the class, I decided to write one too—recounting the octopus episode in full detail. And guess what? The professor chose my composition as the best in the class.

It went something like this:

The Octopus of Huehuete

It was Holy Week, and the sea at Huehuete was calm, its tide pools framed by huge black rocks that looked like ancient guardians. I was there with my sister Elizabeth, invited by the family of her boyfriend, Carlos Jarquín.

Suddenly, as we swam peacefully, a scream tore through the air:

—*"Help! Help me!"* —*It was Elizabeth.*

We rushed toward her, and what we saw looked straight out of a movie: a small octopus had wrapped itself around her leg, clinging with all its tentacles. The creature, stubborn and determined, refused to let go, tightening its grip as if it wanted to drag her into the depths.

Everyone panicked. Some pulled at the tentacles, others shouted without knowing what to do, and Elizabeth kicked in desperation. The octopus, meanwhile, seemed to be enjoying the show—sticking tighter, almost mocking us.

After several frantic attempts, we finally tore it off her leg and hurled it back into the ocean. It flew through the air like a projectile, splashing into the water—a small victory for us all.

There was a strange silence afterward, followed by nervous laughter. Elizabeth, still trembling, checked her leg for marks, while I thought to myself, "This was like an early Easter Sunday—because we almost had heart attacks all around."

A Note to Myself

Who would've thought that a stubborn little octopus would earn me one of my first recognitions as a storyteller!

Chapter 5
The Waterfront

By this stage of my life, I was already *Coca-Cola* in the sports scene—that's how we used to say it, all in one word. (And no, that's not an ad for the soda.) Filin and I had the bad habit of skipping the first class of the day. Instead, we'd sit on a bench at the northwest corner of the Central Park, right across from the rectory where Monsignor Vela Matamoros lived.

We were there for one reason only—to watch our girlfriends, Maritza and Guadalupe, ride by in a horse-drawn carriage on their way to the prestigious Santa Teresita School, one of Masaya's finest private academies. Once they passed, we'd decide whether to head to class at the Institute… or to the market. And to be honest, most of the time we chose the market.

At the market, we'd buy frito and cabeza de chancho—two of Masaya's famous local dishes. Then we'd stop by a cantina, a little bar that sold guaro (a local sugarcane liquor), and pick up a bottle of the famous compuesto de Pablito—a homemade blend, similar to the one my grandfather used to make. The cantina was just two blocks before San Antonio Hospital and half a block to the south.

Loaded up with our "supplies," we'd walk to *El Malecón,* a beautiful park overlooking the Masaya Lagoon. From there, the view was breathtaking—the lagoon shimmering below, the Masaya volcano looming behind it, the high plateau in the distance, and the Pan-American Highway stretching toward Managua, about eighteen miles away. From that same spot, I could see the very path I'd once taken on an old excursion, hiking down from the volcano to the lagoon.

We'd sit under a big tree, open our bottle of Pablito's brew, and between sips, enjoy our meal of traditional food. Not exactly a shining moment—we were a pair of rascals, no doubt about it. Luckily, I still managed to pass the school year, though I only passed one subject: English. At least that one! It would've been the height of irony to fail it.

Then came my third year. Gerardo was already in fourth, while I entered the second-year "A" section at INMA. He was in "B," but that didn't stop us from hanging out all over Masaya. On Sundays, we'd often grab a beer after Mass at the Masaya Theater—right before Gerardo went off to visit his girlfriend, Janette.

Around that time, Gerardo's band, Los Signos del Zodiaco—The Signs of the Zodiac—was starting to make a name for itself. Once, I traveled with them to Estelí, a northern city in Nicaragua, where they had a big gig lined up. Our truck broke down along the way, but Gerardo's grandfather, Don Adán, quickly found another vehicle and got us there, though we arrived a bit late.

When we finally unloaded, I ran into two lovely young women I knew and started chatting with them. Just then, Don Adán appeared. Seeing me idle while the others unloaded the instruments, he scolded me loudly—in front of the girls! I stood there speechless, frozen in embarrassment. After that, Gerardo's brothers, Andrés and Adán, never stopped teasing me about it. In the end, we all ended up laughing until our sides hurt.

Chapter 6
The Insurgent

In my third year of high school, I became friends with a classmate whose name, honestly, I can no longer remember. He often spoke to me about Nicaragua's political turmoil, calling General Anastasio Somoza, then the country's president, a dictator and a murderer who clung to power through violence. He told me that Dr. Pedro Joaquín Chamorro and other prominent political figures, like Dr. Fernando Agüero Rocha, openly opposed the Somoza regime—and that we, as young people, had a duty to take a stand against such injustice.

Yet when I visited Managua, I saw something very different: a city bustling with trade, a growing economy, and cheap prices everywhere. Still, the truth was that the Somoza dynasty had ruled the country since 1934, after the assassination of General Augusto C. Sandino at the hands of Somoza García. My classmate would insist again and again that it was time for the Somozas to pay for all they had done.

Like many rebellious teenagers—between fifteen and nineteen years old—I let myself be influenced. At that age, we're impressionable, drawn to new ideas, and naturally restless with the world around us. That's how I got involved with a small movement of young people eager to see political and social change in Nicaragua.

There were several of us from school, but I especially remember Iván Castellón Bartosh, who introduced me to Mr. Aldo Vega—a well-known and fierce opponent of everything connected to Anastasio Somoza Debayle and the Liberal Party. We would meet in Aldo's house, in a large backyard, where we read revolutionary literature. One of the most striking books we read was Noches de Tortura

(Nights of Torture) by Dr. Clemente Guido, a strong critic of Somoza Debayle. It was a restricted book that described the assassination, in 1956, of General Anastasio Somoza García—the father of Luis and Anastasio Somoza Debayle—and the brutal revenge carried out afterward against anyone suspected of opposition.

Our group grew, and soon our meetings moved to the Malecón of Masaya—the same place where Filin and I used to drink Pablito's homemade brew and eat cabeza de chancho. We were always careful not to be spotted by the National Guard. Between 1970 and 1972, a turbulent time for the country, university and high school students occupied schools, universities, and even Catholic churches in protest against the government—for a range of political and economic reasons.

I, ever the "revolutionary soldier," joined the occupation of INMA and the Church of San Jerónimo, right in my own neighborhood. In my family, I was the only rebel. I remember that one of the protest leaders was named Javier Moncada—a coincidence that caused no small amount of confusion. Dr. Cornelio Hueck, a well-known Somocista politician from Masaya, even called my mother, begging her to keep her son Javier out of "those uprisings." My mother, startled, explained that the rebel was another Javier Moncada—not her son. By God's grace, that misunderstanding saved me from a false accusation.

Even so, my mother asked me to distance myself from those activities. I obeyed—well, halfway. I still joined street demonstrations. During the occupation of INMA, for instance, a group of retired Somocista soldiers, known as the AMROCS, showed up at the gate armed and ready, trying to break in and crush the students. They failed, thanks to the townspeople who gathered outside to stop them. Had they succeeded, it would've ended in a bloodbath.

The national strike lasted about a week until the government finally conceded to several of the protesters' demands—among them, the removal of Father Pallais as rector of the UCA (Central American University).

Chapter 7
Testing, Testing

Continuing the story—still in my third year—I used to pull some outrageous pranks on my teachers. One of my favorites was putting thumbtacks on their chairs, pointy side up, so that when the teacher sat down, they'd jump up yelling, "Ouch! Ouch!" Another trick was spitting on the desk. What a brat I was! I was constantly up to mischief.

I remember once, after one of those stunts, the teacher made the whole class line up in a single file, one behind another, as punishment. He warned us that we'd stay there until someone confessed who had placed the tack and spat on the desk. No one said a word. In silent solidarity with this troublemaker, everyone stood there until three in the afternoon.

I know—it was that wild stage between puberty and adulthood, a wonderful yet rebellious time when we all make foolish mistakes. That's why adults must pay attention to the behavioral changes in teenagers. We've all been there, and we should remember what it felt like. The best thing we can do is guide, advise, and support them—but without yelling or losing our temper.

Looking back now, I realize something: if I had known that most political changes in a country usually boil down to the old saying "Out with you, so I can take your place," I wouldn't have gotten myself "in over my head." As my "Mochito," Rosa Estebana Alfaro Mora—my mother's first cousin and a descendant of Rafaela Herrera—used to say: *"Nobody learns from someone else's experience."*

Faith Beyond the Good, the Bad and the Ugly

By the time I reached my fourth and fifth years, I was going out drinking with friends from all sorts of social backgrounds—usually on weekends. I drank heavily and pushed my physical limits. The Institute had a risky tradition: every year, we'd throw the new high school graduates into the fountains at Central Park, right in front of the school.

In my fifth year, I experimented with sleeping pills and marijuana. Thank God, I didn't like them; I preferred alcohol instead. But now I know that neither one does you any good. It was the era of rock music, hippies, and free love.

In fourth year, during a school trip to the Masaya Volcano, we traveled on the school's bus, driven by the official inspector-chauffeur. When the excursion ended, the bus was supposed to meet us for the return trip—but it never showed up. We waited nearly three hours. Finally, we decided to walk the eight kilometers back to Masaya.

When we were about two kilometers from the city, near Nindirí, the bus finally appeared. The driver asked us to get on, but we refused—we had already walked far enough, and it felt like a matter of respect. Our protest reached the school's administrative council, where we demanded his dismissal. We elected a student, Jims Sandoval (may he rest in peace), to represent us, with a single mission: to request the driver's removal.

But Jims accepted a different deal with the council, which handed down only a light punishment. The issue was soon forgotten, and Jims never represented the students again. Later, we found out why—he was the driver's brother-in-law.

Chapter 8
High School Graduation – Passion

At last, graduation day arrived! We all marched proudly in a grand ceremony at INMA. Each student walked alongside their parents—the girls with their fathers, and the boys with their mothers. It was the 25th graduating class, the "Manuel Rocha Marenco" Promotion, and about fifteen pairs of siblings graduated together that year.

To celebrate, we went to Tip Top Restaurant, owned by the Rosales family in Masaya. Among us were Roger Abaunza, Rodolfo *"Pepe"* Miranda Escobar, Donald and Aníbal Noguera, and me.

Of course, once I entered university, I kept living at the same pace. When I broke up with my girlfriend, Odilie, I fell into a depression—*what we call cavanga back home*—but I've already told that story, along with my mother's wise advice that helped me through it. Even so, that sadness never led me to excessive drinking; I only drank occasionally.

By my third semester at the university, life took a turn toward passion—my sensuality awakened like a rocket taking off. Thank goodness I didn't become a priest! After classes, I divided my time between my girlfriend and my professors, who sometimes invited me out for a drink. With my girlfriend—who was working while studying—we'd go to some of the best restaurants in Managua, and afterward…

I'm sorry, Patricia. This is my story—what I lived through. You know well that you are the one chosen by God for me, just as I was chosen for you.

Chapter 9
The Consequence of Liquor

In my fourth year of university, after leaving the house of my mentor, Engineer Roberto Fajardo, we had been drinking—he, my friend Javier Will, and I. By the time we left, we were all more than a little drunk. I dropped Will off at his house and then headed toward Masaya in my little Fiat.

When I reached Nindirí, I came across a large freight truck that had broken down and was parked carelessly right in my lane. I turned the wheel hard to the left, trying to avoid it, but it was too late. The front right side of my car slammed into the truck's platform, sending me—and the car—flying into the opposite lane. By God's grace, there were no vehicles coming from the other direction. My car bounced three times from the impact, but it didn't flip over. Had it rolled, that would've been the end of me. As we say in Nicaragua, "it just wasn't my time yet."

I managed to straighten the car and continue driving, though the grinding metal noise betrayed the extent of the damage, until I reached the garage where I parked it. When I inspected the car, the right headlight, fender, front grill, and several other parts were gone. That little "lesson" cost me about $1,500—a lot of money back then.

When I got home, the first thing I did was confess to my mother. She spoke to me with such tenderness and love that I didn't feel ashamed of the accident itself, but rather humbled by the immense love she showed me—love I felt I didn't deserve.

Faith Beyond the Good, the Bad and the Ugly

By the end of my fourth year, during the second semester of 1978, the political situation in the country had reached a boiling point. Nicaragua was erupting like one of its fourteen volcanoes, following the assassination of Dr. Pedro Joaquín Chamorro. In protest, universities were occupied, and I took part in the takeover of the UCA, serving as a member of the student council. I remember being there alongside Adrián Meza, Carlos Velázquez, Óscar Miranda, Alejandro Pérez Arévalo Jr., Miriam Ramírez Hebe, and many other students. The strike lasted about fifteen days.

During those turbulent years—1977 and 1978—whenever I drove from Managua to visit my girlfriend and then continued on to Masaya, usually after ten at night, I often found myself caught in the middle of clashes between FSLN commandos and the National Guard. More than once, I drove my little Fiat through bursts of gunfire until I reached the house where I parked. From there, I had to cross through neighbors' yards to get home safely.

I saw the bullets with my own eyes—at night, you could clearly see the sparks flash from the barrels as they fired. I lived through that kind of chaos many times, never knowing when the FSLN insurgents would attack in Masaya.

And as we like to say back home, *"a pair of breasts can pull harder than a cart full of oxen."*

Chapter 10
The Sale of My House

In 1984, I was working at the Javier Guerra Sugar Mill. My father and I were living together in my house—I call it mine because it was the house where I was born, and I always believed that, being the youngest son, it would one day belong to me. It was the house with the big backyard, the one my father eventually decided not to keep, wanting to avoid disputes with the neighbors who lived behind the property.

The house was in my father's name, not mine. For reasons I still don't understand, he suddenly became convinced that selling it was the right thing to do. My brother Miguel made him an offer, but my father refused. If only he had accepted, the property would have stayed within the family. But no—he sold it to a man who worked at a commercial bank.

I then moved into my grandparents' house, which was right next door to the one that had just been sold. I only remember asking my father:

—*"Are you sure about what you're doing?"*

And he answered, yes.

That was it—I lost my home. It was gone. And I must admit, my mind wasn't clear either. I was going through a rough time: recently separated from the mother of my son, César Ricardo; under pressure to prove myself capable of handling the sugar mill's challenges; in love with Patricia while her father was waging war against me; and, on top of all that, drinking too much. I didn't have the clarity or the strength to deal with the situation, much less to stop the sale.

What happened later with my grandparents' house, the Moncada home, I'll tell you in Part III: The Ugly.

Chapter 11
In Prison

On March 19, 1985, I was violently taken from my office, where I was leading the Harvest Council at the Javier Guerra Sugar Mill. Four soldiers stormed in and forced me into a Soviet-made UAZ jeep, each one armed and keeping watch over me. I was speechless, trying to understand what this outrage meant.

They took me to the military barracks in Nandaime and ordered me to sit on a bench "while they waited for further orders." Many people saw me there, among them Leonor Dumas, who worked for my future mother-in-law, Doña Nelly León—and later for Patricia and me. She immediately informed Doña Nelly, who then told Patricia, my girlfriend.

After about an hour and a half, they transferred me to the Police Processing Center in the city of Granada, about twenty kilometers away. There I remained for nearly two weeks, locked up with common criminals. I had no idea why I'd been arrested—no explanation, no charges, nothing.

Midway through that week, Patricia, her mother, and her sister María Leonor—whom we all affectionately called Nonga—tried to visit me. I found out because a soldier came to my cell and said,

—"Your girlfriend came to see you, but you're incommunicado. What a pity—she's so beautiful, and you won't get to have her."

In that moment, I felt completely defeated. It was psychological torture.

Faith Beyond the Good, the Bad and the Ugly

The cell offered no privacy. About twenty of us were crammed into a small space. The latrine had no door, not even a toilet—just a hole in the ground. Next to it, high on the wall, was a pipe that served as a shower.

One night, they took me into a separate room for interrogation. They wanted to know if certain sugar mill officials were stealing and how they did it. I stood silent—what were they even talking about?

—"Listen," one said, "if you cooperate with us, we'll treat you well—and maybe you'll get out."

His words reminded me of something that had happened the year before. In 1984, the FSLN's political branch in my region—Region IV—had tried to recruit me to go fight in the mountains against the armed counterrevolution. They nearly succeeded. They even promised that, when I returned, I could become General Manager of the sugar mill. When Engineer Eduardo Holman Chamorro, the Regional Director of MIDINRA, heard about it, he sent word telling me to forget such nonsense—that my real battlefield was the Production Department. What a relief that was. I had almost been convinced.

Back to the interrogation: since they didn't get the answers they wanted, they attacked me emotionally, talking about Patricia—saying I'd never see her again, that she'd marry someone else, and so on.

Later, they moved me from Police Processing to La Granja Prison—still without formal charges. La Granja was a wooden structure with two large wings enclosed in wire mesh, like an oversized chicken coop—hence the name. The wing I was in had three cells: one for military prisoners who had violated their own laws, and two for common inmates. The other entire wing was for hardened criminals. My cell was between the first two, housing about forty prisoners.

Every day we were taken to the yard for roll call—three or four times a day, as I later learned, to make sure no one had escaped. When we spoke to a soldier, we had to say, "Comrade combatant," and respond, "Yes, comrade combatant!"

We were allowed to bathe once a week, at four in the morning. Our water came from a horizontal iron tank, flush with the ground, open at the top. From that same tank, we drank. One day, they asked for volunteers to clean it. I volunteered, just for the chance to wash myself. Inside, to my horror, it was full of worms. And that was the same water I had been drinking all along.

Once a week, we were taken to the nearby hills to collect firewood for the kitchen—heavily guarded, of course. The guards told us that prisoners had no citizen rights and that, if the U.S. attacked Nicaragua, we'd be the first to be executed.

The "bathrooms" were twelve holes in a row, about a meter apart, with no walls or partitions—everyone in full view of everyone else. If someone needed to relieve himself outside of the scheduled time, he had to do it behind the cell and wrap it in newspaper. Once, I went there without really needing to, forced myself—and fainted. They took me to the infirmary, and that's how I got a look at more of the facility. There, I saw the military prisoners building the new concrete prison that would soon replace La Granja.

While in Processing, I wrote several letters to Patricia and my brother Miguel, asking them to contact Jorge Correa and Jims Sandoval, both lawyers—Jorge, a great friend, and Jims, a classmate from high school.

When I was finally called to court for my charges to be read, my brother Miguel came to fetch me from La Granja and take me to Granada. Jorge came along, as did my sister-in-law Tere and a guard. On the way, I asked Jorge,

—"What exactly am I being accused of?"

"Embezzlement, conspiracy, and abuse of trust," he replied.

—*"In short, what does that mean?"*

—*"Theft from the State."*

—*"And how many years is that?"*

—*"At least seven."*

I was stunned. "But I haven't done any of that," I told him.

At the courthouse, I found myself face to face with José Díaz, General Manager of the mill; the Administrator; the Field Chief, Hernán Membreño; the mill's buyer, Mr. Amador; and the union leaders Diógenes Carranza and Vanegas. All of them were under arrest, charged with the same crimes.

Our lawyers explained that the FSLN's political branch in Region IV had pressured authorities to arrest professionals from state-confiscated companies: the Javier Guerra Sugar Mill, MICONS, PLASTINIC, and ENABAS. It was a political move meant to discredit us.

In the case of Javier Guerra, Engineer Miguel Gómez—a colleague of mine, and my former professor of Thermal Machines at the university—had filed the complaint, though under pressure. In his testimony, however, he spoke in my favor. Gómez had recently replaced Engineer Eduardo Holman as Regional Director of MIDINRA, since Eduardo had been promoted to Vice Minister.

My lawyer, Jims Sandoval, requested that several key witnesses be called to testify for me: Engineer Edgar Vargas (Director of Nicaragua's Sugar Industry), Miguel Gómez himself, and Engineer David Morice (Administrator of Ingenio San Antonio). All three gave strong, unanimous testimony about my professional integrity and work at Javier Guerra.

The prosecution, on the other hand, brought in a few workers. During the judge's questioning, one said, "Engineer Julio Moncada drinks a lot—he drives around in the state vehicle with a driver and once bit a secretary on the cheek." That ridiculous accusation made everyone burst out laughing—even the Sandinista judge.

I was imprisoned for three months. On May 30, 1985, Judge Agustín issued a full acquittal and ordered the release of all the detainees. The FSLN's political figures opposed the ruling, but the judge stood firm. We walked out of La Granja on June 3. Patricia, her mother, and Nonga came to pick me up and take me to Nandaime. From that day on, I lived in one of my future mother-in-law's houses. My grandmother Julia remained in her own home until she passed away.

Soon after, Engineer Edgar Vargas invited me to work for the National Sugar Directorate. When no one from MIDINRA came forward to apologize for what they'd done to me, my lifelong mentor, Dr. Jaime Downing, called Edgar personally and asked that I be reassigned to POLYCASA. He even called me in Nandaime, having tracked down *Doña* Nelly's phone number himself.

I accepted the offer and went to work under Dr. Downing as Plant Chief (the Production Manager then was Engineer Tomás Urroz, who had replaced me back in 1980 when I left for ATCHEMCO). I worked with Dr. Downing for six months, but I could see the company was being hit by international sanctions and losing its status as a Central American leader. To avoid hurting anyone's feelings, I told him I planned to go to Mexico to pursue a master's in distillation—and I suggested that POLYCASA's plant could be adapted to produce alcohol and that its PVC resin dryer could also be used to dry sugar. Then I called Edgar Vargas to ask if the position at the Sugar Directorate was still open.

—*"Hurry up,"* he said. *"The sooner, the better."*

Chapter 12
The Theft

When I began working at the Javier Guerra Sugar Mill, I was already a heavy drinker. And sugar mills were no exception—whether in Nicaragua, Cuba, Mexico, or later in the United States during 1991 and 1992, drinking seemed to be part of the culture.

However, in 1994, I made a firm decision to quit drinking altogether, and I kept that promise for fifteen years. I broke it again in 2010, by then living in the United States—but only occasionally and lightly, nothing like before.

In 2004, while in Miami Beach, I parked my car in a public street parking area. When I came back, I found the driver's-side window smashed and my backpack stolen—with all my important documents inside: driver's license, Social Security card, credit cards, and more.

I immediately called the credit card companies to report the theft and—can you believe it?—the thieves had already used them! All the cards were promptly canceled.

The strangest part was that I ended up driving without a license—from Pahokee to the Okeelanta Sugar Mill—for almost five years.

One of my coworkers told me he had managed to fix his legal status through political asylum, with help from an organization calling itself the Protocathedral of the Catholic Church, supposedly run by a man named Peter. But it turned out to have nothing at all to do with the real Catholic Church.

Chapter 13
Peter and USCIS

To resolve my immigration status—and that of my entire family, since Bryan had already been born in 2006—I attended a conference in October 2008 led by a man named Peter. The first requirement was to attend a Sunday Mass celebrated by him. That's when we discovered that Peter wasn't actually a priest—he was a married man, a grandfather.

At the end of the Mass, everyone had to sign a registration book to be allowed into his conference. The session lasted four straight hours, during which Peter talked nonstop, explaining how to obtain U.S. residency through an asylum petition. He had a team of assistants and lawyers who seemed to know the process well. For his services, he charged a "modest" fee of $300. At the time, it didn't seem unreasonable. I agreed, and we began the process.

First, we filled out a draft of the asylum application form for USCIS. Then his team typed up the official paperwork to be filed formally. Once the application was submitted, the 150-day waiting period began before I could apply for a work permit.

In 2009, I was called in by USCIS for an interview with an asylum officer. During the questioning, the officer asked about my Social Security card, my work permit, and where I was employed. I told him everything exactly as it was—no lies, no evasions. I knew that if you lie in front of an immigration officer, "whoosh, you're cooked," because they miss nothing.

He asked for my work permit, looked at it, and said immediately,

—*"This is fake."*

I was stunned. I had no idea it wasn't genuine—remember, dear reader, how I'd gotten it years earlier. The officer, however, said,

—"Because you haven't lied and you've told the whole truth, we'll give you another interview. Just explain where and how you met Mr. Richard, the Haitian. Your time will continue to count—we won't stop the process."

At the second interview, I submitted all the information they requested. When the 150 days were up, I was able to begin the process of obtaining new work permits, Social Security cards, and driver's licenses. The joy in my family was immense! They say almost no one gets such a second chance with Immigration—but we never stopped praying. Was it God's hand at work? Dear reader, you can answer that for yourself.

And look how the Lord works: the very next day after receiving my first USCIS work permit in the mail, I got a call from Mr. Báez, the Human Resources Manager at Okeelanta. He told me that my work permit had expired—six years earlier!—and that I needed to prove my legal status immediately. At that moment, I was in Miami with Patricia and my sister-in-law, María Leonor—our dear "Nonga." We drove straight to Okeelanta, and I showed him my brand-new permit. Báez examined it carefully and confirmed it was legitimate. Rumors had been spreading that I was undocumented. What a relief! Thank God! That was in 2010.

My work permit was renewed each year. In 2011, a setback occurred—perhaps due to an oversight by my lawyer. Okeelanta called, asking me to bring in my new permit because the old one had expired. I went to see Báez and explained the situation. With great generosity, he told me to take all the time I needed and assured me that my job would be waiting for me once my new permit arrived. A true blessing from God. That kind of understanding is rare in the U.S.—unless you have powerful backing… but I knew my backing came from God Himself.

We had to restart the process from the beginning. We returned to Immigration Court, where the honorable Judge Illeana Torrez-Bayouth granted us permission to continue receiving work permits while our asylum petition was under review. After seven months of waiting, the renewed permit finally arrived in the mail. I went back to Okeelanta, and Báez reinstated me as Production Supervisor.

I should note that during those seven months, all household expenses were covered by my children, who were already working and contributed generously. Patricia also cooked nacatamales—that delicious traditional Nicaraguan dish—which I sold every Thursday to refinery workers, with full authorization from Okeelanta's top management. That way, we kept our household afloat. I also used those Thursdays to show up in person, reminding everyone that I was still committed to my position—because there were many professionals and engineers eager to take my place. The blessing was that Okeelanta waited for me.

During that time, Father John offered us financial help, but guided by the Holy Spirit, I thanked him and declined. I told him we trusted entirely in Divine Providence. And that's exactly how it turned out—Emmanuel!

I share all this to show the trials and anguish we went through during those eighteen years, in which, year after year—and later every two—I renewed my work permit under category C(8), meaning "asylum pending." Finally, by the grace of God, in 2023, Patricia and I were able to obtain our permanent legal status through our son's petition.

Today, with my children all professionals and three of them married, I can proudly say they followed a principle we always taught them:

first graduate, then marry. And they kept their word—examples of discipline and responsibility.

Chapter 14
My Retirement

I probably shouldn't have retired… though I can't say I regret it either. That's a common thought after leaving one's job, because retirement is a completely different chapter of life. A married man suddenly spends twenty-four hours a day with his wife—especially if, like mine, she's a homemaker—and a single man often grows restless quickly. Fortunately, that wasn't my case.

Of the eighteen years I worked at Okeelanta, I spent only two Christmases and New Year's with my family—and not even consecutive ones. During the early years, the most senior supervisor had the right to take vacation in December, and one of my coworkers took advantage of that for six straight years, until he retired. Then, the next in line took those holidays for three more years before his own retirement.

Because of these complications, the company decided to rotate December vacations starting from the most senior. I ended up second on the list. Eventually, management ruled that no Production Supervisor could take time off in December at all—vacations would have to be distributed during other months of the year.

The only two times I managed to spend the holidays with my family were thanks to the shift schedule rotation. Each month, supervisors had seven days off, divided into blocks of one, two, and four days. In 2017, the rotation happened to give me four free days exactly during the Christmas and New Year season. However, a newly hired supervisor requested those same dates as vacation. I was called into a meeting with Báez, and they asked me to give up my scheduled days off so the new supervisor could take them. Of course, I had no real choice but to agree. I simply told Báez, firmly and clearly:

—*"May 30, 2018, will be my last day of work. That day, I retire."*

And that's exactly how it happened. My final week on the job was a night shift—from 11 p.m. to 7 a.m.—and each night, I said my goodbyes with pride and satisfaction, knowing I had done my duty well.

I retired at 62 and a half, applied for Social Security Retirement, and waited until I turned 65 to enroll in Medicare, just as the law requires.

I also want to remember an important episode: in 2004, the workers at Okeelanta went on strike. The supervisors had to keep the sugar production going without interruption, taking over all the tasks normally handled by the laborers. It was about four intense days, but we did an excellent job. We organized two shifts: I led the night shift, from 7 p.m. to 7 a.m., while the day shift—from 7 a.m. to 7 p.m.—was led by Engineer Alejandro Morales, who today serves as the General Manager of the refinery.

Chapter 15
My Free Time

(Flagstaff – Albuquerque)

At the end of 2018, we all took a family trip to California. Oh, and before I forget—Okeelanta gave me a farewell gift for my 18 years of service: a carry-on suitcase, a beautiful Seiko watch, and, of course, my retirement compensation, which I requested as a lump sum. Nothing extraordinary, but fair and appreciated.

Patricia, Bryan, and I traveled by car; the rest of the family flew. The following year, I bought another ticket in advance for California—but guess what? By the time of the flight, my work permit renewal still hadn't arrived. So we had to split up: Patricia went with the girls and Bryan by plane, while Julio Jr., Gonzalo, and I made the trip by road.

As we drove through Flagstaff, Arizona, we saw snow for the first time. I told Julio to pull over so we could touch it and play a little. We stopped at an intersection, but before we could get out, a police car parked right next to us. The officer explained that we couldn't stop there—it was a designated emergency zone. I tried to explain that we were from Florida and had never seen snow before. But he firmly said he needed to speak with the driver, not me. I immediately slid back into my seat because my documents were expired and awaiting renewal. The outcome: Julio got the ticket.

When we reached Albuquerque, New Mexico, we stayed at a Hilton hotel. That same night, in the hotel parking lot, thieves broke the rear left window of the car and stole my laptop and a guitar I was carrying as a favor for Patricia's cousin, Elia María. What a blow!

How could I tell Elia that her guitar had been stolen? Would she even believe me? To this day, I'm not entirely sure she did.

Once we got to California, we stayed at the home of Braxis, Patricia's sister, in the city of Milpitas. Patricia, Bryan, and I stayed there for three months, while the rest of the family flew back to Florida earlier. During that time, we got to play in the snow at a recreational park near Reno, Lake Tahoe, Nevada.

We had actually visited that same place back in 1991, during one of our earlier vacations. Finally, we drove back to Florida in February 2020—just before the Covid-19 pandemic broke out.

Chapter 16
A Few Things I Did in My Free Time

(Oxbridge – PBMA – Craft Beer)

In October 2022, by pure blessing, I began working at Oxbridge Academy as an on-call substitute teacher—a short-term position. And I say "by pure blessing" because my son, Julio César, had previously worked at that same institution as a long-term substitute during the pandemic (2020–2021), teaching Spanish in place of Mrs. María Morice, a dear friend of ours.

When I applied, they initially assumed I was my son, but the confusion was quickly cleared up. Fortunately, Julio had done an excellent job, and his reputation opened the door for me. That school year, I was called only a few times—once a week, sometimes twice, and on a good week, three times. The best part was the chemistry I developed with the students, though I was hoping for something more stable.

For the 2023–2024 school year, I applied to another institution: Palm Beach Maritime Academy (PBMA). My plan was to combine both schools so I could work the entire week. PBMA's General Manager of Human Resources, Anthony Andrepont, a friend of Julio César Jr., asked him if he had applied. Julio told him no—it was his father. Anthony replied, "If you're such a fine young man and a great person, your dad must be even better. Tell him to come—he's got a job."

I went through the full application and interview process—just as I had at Oxbridge—and I understood that my position was full time.

I interpreted that to mean permanent and with benefits, but later I found out that wasn't quite the case. Still, I built a great rapport with the students.

Things got complicated when the 7th and 8th-grade Math teacher went on leave. The Middle School and Upper School principals asked me to take over his classes. I asked whether my pay would be adjusted to that of a full-time teacher, but they said they weren't sure. Trusting they'd sort it out, I accepted. A month and a half went by with no change in pay.

At that point, I decided to schedule all my medical appointments and informed PBMA that I'd be out for about a week and a half. I set the appointments for afternoons so I could keep substituting at Oxbridge, and I also took a few extra days off when Patricia fell ill.

At PBMA, I kept covering classes: first for the World History teacher for a month, then for the 6th-grade Science teacher for three weeks. Eventually, I realized I couldn't keep up that juggling act; I had to choose between the two schools. It was a hard decision because I received the same warmth and respect from both: one, an elite private academy; the other, a public charter school. But the affection I felt from the students was identical.

The day I made my choice, I tried to reach Anthony but couldn't get through. I left a message with his assistant and never found out if she passed it along—because I never went back to PBMA. Ironically, I kept running into Anthony afterward at St. Thomas More Church, but we never spoke about it.

In the end, I continued at Oxbridge until October 2024, when my time there came to a close.

Then, in June 2024, I discovered a new passion: brewing homemade craft beer. The reception was fantastic. Making this kind of beer is absolutely fascinating—anyone can do it, as long as they're extremely careful about cleanliness and preventing contamination. There's plenty of literature available on the process, and every batch is a brand-new world, full of learning and discovery.

Chapter 17: My Left Knee

Back in my soccer-playing days, during a training session with my youth team and some players from Deportivo Chávez—a First Division club in Nicaragua—two of them were joking around, tossing a large rock back and forth. Just as I happened to walk by, unaware of their "game," the rock struck me squarely on the left knee. The impact was brutal; my knee swelled up like a balloon.

They rushed over to help, clearly worried, but the damage was already done. I didn't tell my mother a thing, knowing she would have banned me from ever playing soccer again. Every night, I massaged the knee with a liniment for bruises and gradually managed to bring down the swelling and pain. Still, as the years went by, that injury would come back to haunt me.

In my youth, I never felt any further pain. But years later, while working at Okeelanta, I suffered several falls—including one serious tumble down the stairs from the second floor of my home in Pahokee. X-rays revealed bad news: my knee had no meniscus left, no cartilage; the kneecap was literally grinding bone against bone. The doctors concluded that the only real solution was a total knee replacement with a metal prosthesis.

That was in 2016. I sought a second opinion, but the diagnosis was the same. Fear got the better of me, and I decided to keep going—at that time, the pain wasn't limiting my movements too much. But when Bryan started playing soccer and I'd join him on the field, the pain and occasional falls began. At night, I'd feel discomfort and sharp twinges that slowly turned into constant pain.

From 2016 until 2024, I endured it. But in October of that year, after finishing my time at Oxbridge, I made the decision—it was time to have the surgery. I spent two months thinking it through, completed all the necessary tests, and had a pre-surgical interview at the hospital.

The operation took place on January 8, 2025, performed by Dr. Harvey Montijo. It lasted about two hours. Thanks to the anesthesia, I didn't feel a thing. When I woke up, I was already in the recovery room at Palm Beach Gardens Hospital, my left leg immobilized, wrapped in heavy bandages, and fitted with a support brace.

They gave me so many pills that the nurse joked they called it "the cocktail of pills." The entire staff treated me with kindness and care. On the second day, Dr. Montijo's trusted therapist came in, helped me out of bed, made me walk with a walker, and even taught me how to get into a car properly. That same afternoon, I was discharged and sent home.

The next day, I had a follow-up appointment with Dr. Montijo. He removed the brace, leaving just the bandage, and asked if I preferred to start my first two weeks of therapy at home or directly at the clinic. I told him I'd rather begin at home to get adjusted. That's how I started my recovery, with three therapy sessions a week under the care of Abby Sargent, a dedicated and compassionate therapist. The exercises were familiar—just like soccer warm-ups—but this time, I was working with a prosthetic instead of a natural knee.

Once that stage was completed, I continued therapy at PT Bone & Joint Surgery, where I was attended by Ana Pedridin, Lance Morris, Sebastián, and Frances—a wonderful team of professionals. My last session there was on June 12, 2025. That day, Ana told me that, according to protocol, I had regained about 85–90% of my mobility.

On June 17, I had another check-up with Dr. Montijo. He showed me the X-rays of both knees and confirmed that everything looked excellent, especially considering I was only five months post-surgery. He decided to extend therapy for six more weeks, two sessions per week.

Today, seven months after surgery, I feel great. There's still a little pain and mild swelling, but the doctor assures me that's normal at this stage. And the best part: I can dance salsa, cumbia, and merengue again!

Spiritual Reflection

Through this entire process, I confirmed once more that God never abandons those who trust in Him. From that childhood injury to the surgery and recovery, His powerful hand has been with me every step of the way. Today, I can say that the prosthesis in my knee is also a reminder that the Lord renews us, sustains us, and gives us new chances to keep walking in His path.

Glory to God, who allowed me to rise, recover, and continue enjoying life, my family, and the joy of dancing once more!

PARTE III
THE UGLY

There's a Nicaraguan saying that goes, "Aquello que no es chicha ni es limonada," which literally means "something that's neither corn drink nor lemonade." But what it really means is something in-between—something that doesn't quite fit on either side. Neither one thing nor the other.

And that, dear reader, is how I'd describe certain moments in life—those confusing, gray areas where you don't know whether to laugh or cry, stay or go, speak or stay silent. I've lived a few of those seasons myself. Times when faith tells you one thing, but reason whispers another. When you're not falling, but you're not standing tall either.

It's in those moments that God often does His quietest work. You can't see it, you can't name it—it's not chicha or limonada—but it's grace in motion, shaping your heart in silence.

Chapter 1
White Boots

Ever since I was little, I was a bit of a show-off —a real dandy. One Christmas, I put on my brand-new outfit, feeling sharp, and lit a Roman candle —those metal sticks wrapped with gunpowder that shoot sparks like mini fireworks. With the candle blazing, I lowered my right hand, holding it near my knee... and guess what? I burned a hole right through my new pants! I had to cut them off and turn them into shorts. They looked awful!

In fifth grade, my classmate Rigoberto Cabezas Boza —who later became one of my best friends and my fellow high school graduate— used to tease me endlessly because I wore a pair of white boots with a small heel.

Now, those boots had a story of their own. My grandmother María, after returning from a vacation trip to the United States, stayed with us as she always did. She brought back a bunch of gifts, and among them were those boots —the moment I saw them, I fell in love. I asked her for them, but she told me they were women's boots. Still enchanted by how soft the leather felt and how perfectly they fit, I told her it didn't matter —they could be for men too, they were "unisex."

Big mistake! From that day on, Rigo wouldn't stop teasing me about it. Eventually, I had to stop wearing them, even hiding my feet so the girls wouldn't notice. What an embarrassing memory... but it makes me laugh now!

Looking back, I think many people probably remember me in those white boots —and beyond all the teasing, they were my first bold attempt to express my own style.

Chapter 2
Encounter with Dina

After graduating as a dentist in Mexico, my brother Javier moved to the United States, where my mamatía lived, to continue studying and practicing his profession. There he met Dolores, who would later become his wife.

Some time later, Javier came back to Nicaragua for vacation and to visit the family. One afternoon, we were all gathered at my brother Miguel's house —he was also a dentist who had studied in Mexico. As was the custom back home, we sat outside on the sidewalk and partly on the street, chatting, watching people go by, and greeting our neighbors.

Suddenly, Mrs. Dina Bermúdez drove past in her car (she lived not far from Miguel's place). When she recognized Javier, she stopped, got out, and greeted him enthusiastically. Then she greeted all of us and started chatting with him… in English! They talked for quite a while before she finally said goodbye to everyone and drove away.

And guess what? She didn't even look at me —as if I didn't exist! Of course, how could she? She was the same English teacher I had once thrown an eraser at back in school… She never forgot!

What an awkward, cringeworthy encounter that was.

That day I confirmed what I'd always suspected: teachers never forget —especially their most unbearable students.

Chapter 3
My Grandfather's House

Between 1993 and 1998, while I was in the business of selling aguardiente, I asked my father to transfer to me the house that had once belonged to my grandfather, Deogracias. He agreed and did so.

With that property now in my name, I decided to set up my business there in Masaya. To finance it, I applied for a bank loan, using the house as collateral. However, by the end of July 1999, an unexpected trip to the United States came up. Faced with that situation, I made an arrangement with the bank and with Dr. Carlos Cárdenas (may he rest in peace), who agreed to pay off the loan. Once the debt was settled, the house would become his.

I also sold my vehicle—a Chevrolet Astro Van—which I had bought in the United States during one of my vacation trips back in 1992.

Twenty-five years later, during one of my three visits to Nicaragua, I took Bryan David with me, full of nostalgia, to see my old houses: the first, where I was born, still stands just as I left it; and the second, my paternal grandparents' house, where I also lived. A new house has now been built there.

On the part of the property my grandfather once sold to Violeta—my father's cousin—her daughter Brenda now lives. She's the only one who stayed in Nicaragua, since Violeta emigrated to the United States with all her children many years ago.

As I showed those homes to Bryan, I realized that what we truly inherit is not walls or roofs, but memories and roots—things that time can never erase.

Chapter 4
ATCHEMCO

The Compañía Química de la Costa Atlántica (ATCHEMCO), or Atlantic Coast Chemical Company, was a Nicaraguan enterprise managed by American and Cuban engineers close to the government of Anastasio Somoza Debayle. It was founded as part of an ambitious Central American Economic Integration plan promoted by INFONAC (Industria y Fomento Nacional), the national agency responsible for bringing new industries into the country. Among those were ATCHEMCO, ELPESA (Electroquímica Penwalt), Borden Chemical, and HERCASA (Hércules de Centroamérica), among others.

ATCHEMCO was established on Nicaragua's northern Atlantic coast, where pine trees—the company's main raw material—were abundant. For every tree cut down, five were planted to preserve the local flora and fauna. The plant was located in La Tronquera, Lecus Creek, in the region of Northern Zelaya.

Back then, ground access was extremely limited; the most reliable way to get there was by air, through Puerto Cabezas. The company even had its own twin-engine, eight-passenger aircraft to transport staff and executives. It also operated a cargo ship—the Cherylen—stationed at the port of Lamlaya, which was responsible for exporting finished products abroad.

During my time there, my colleague José Luis and I, along with a few local guides, would often go on night hunts deep in the Atlantic jungle. It was common to hear the roars of lions, ocelots, and panthers. We hunted deer and iguanas so large they looked like small alligators. In the rivers, we caught groupers, and at depths as tall as two men, we found oysters. Sometimes we even spotted stingrays and small sharks venturing from the ocean into the river mouths where we navigated in motorized pangas (small boats). The most awe-inspiring of all those trips was along the Coco River—immense and majestic.

I remember one particular incident: after spending some time in Waspam, we were driving back to La Tronquera. I was at the wheel and missed a turn, ending up in a deep ditch along the gravel road. When I finally managed to pull the Suburban—a well-equipped seven-seater—out of the ditch, we realized all four tires had gone flat. José Luis, frustrated, grabbed an AK-47 and emptied the entire magazine into the air. We eventually had to call for help over the radio.

Life at ATCHEMCO was a strange paradox. In the middle of the jungle, the houses of the technical staff and engineers were true dream homes—comfortable, modern, and luxurious. Today, their value would easily exceed half a million dollars. It was surreal to see such wealth in such isolation—a clear reflection of the company's political backing and financial power.

"In those years, I came to understand that ATCHEMCO was more than just a factory; it was a symbol of contrast—between progress and neglect, between the luxury of a few and the harshness of the jungle that surrounded it."

Chapter 5
Renting Homes

Throughout my professional life, I've rented many houses—ever since 1982. The first was a lovely home near Nindirí, close to Masaya.

When Patricia and I got married, we lived twice in Managua. The first time was in Barrio El Carmen, near where President Daniel Ortega currently resides. We eventually moved back to Nandaime because of the political unrest that followed the election victory of Doña Violeta de Chamorro in 1990.

The second time, we lived near the Plaza España roundabout, but we had to return to Nandaime again after a break-in occurred while Patricia and the girls were in the United States and I was attending a sugar industry conference in Costa Rica. Altogether, our time renting in Managua added up to about three years. The rest of the time, we lived with my in-laws.

We spent one year on my father-in-law's farm in Catarina—which has since been taken over—and then rented a house across from my mother-in-law's, owned by one of Patricia's aunts. We stayed there for another year, until we finally left for the United States.

In the U.S., our first home was in Pahokee, where we rented three different houses:

- The first one, where we lived for six years (2000–2006), and even had snakes show up inside.
- The second, where we stayed for less than two years.

- And the third, where we spent ten years—from 2008 until my retirement in 2018.

In October of that same year, we moved to West Palm Beach, to a house where we stayed for two years. However, we soon discovered it had too many issues. Finally, in November 2019—right before the pandemic—we moved into our current home, located between Lake Worth and Boynton Beach, still within West Palm Beach.

In summary: five rented houses in Nicaragua and five in the United States over forty years of marriage—an average of about four years per house.

Do we own property in the U.S.? Not yet… but I'm still hopeful!

"Beyond all the moves and changes of address, what truly sustained us was the home we built together as a family—because in the end, real ownership lies in love and unity."

Chapter 6
Buying Cars

EThe first car I ever bought was when I was working as an assistant at the UCA: a yellow, two-door FIAT 127. It was a great little car. I bought it used in 1976, with my brother Miguel co-signing the loan—at my mother's insistence—since he already had his dental clinic set up thanks to her.

In 1980, I sold it to Engineer Guido and bought myself a brand-new Mazda 323. Then, in 1983, I made the mistake of selling that one to buy a used Cherokee Indian, which I later sold to some international journalists. With that money, I bought a used AMC Concord.

Of course, once I started working at the sugar mills, I was always assigned a company jeep with a driver.

In 1992, during a trip to San Francisco, California, I bought a Chevrolet Astro Van from one of Patricia's uncles. Later, I traded it to the distillery at the Montelimar sugar mill. After that, I bought a single-cabin Mitsubishi pickup, and when I sold it, I purchased a semi-new Toyota Hilux with four doors. I had an accident with that truck; once repaired, I sold it and switched to a used Nissan Patrol, which I drove to La Grecia Sugar Mill in Honduras.

On a return trip to Nicaragua, I sold that one and bought a Jeep Cherokee. Back in Honduras, I got myself a Toyota Station Wagon with dual transmission. In 1996, I sold both vehicles and bought two brand-new ones: a four-door Nissan and a Mitsubishi Montero.

(At this point, don't even bother counting... I lost track myself! And that's not even including the cars I bought in the U.S.)

In the U.S., the first was an Audi—but it had a bad transmission, so I got rid of it and bought a Dodge Van for 300 dollars. I later gave that van to a family in need and got another Dodge Van. After that came a Ford Winstar (which ended up as a junk car), a 2001 Chevrolet Tahoe, and four cars for my kids: a Nissan Sentra, a Toyota Corolla, a manual-transmission Ford Focus, and a Toyota Tercel.

Later on, we added a Ford F-350 diesel, an Infiniti QX-50, and three Mitsubishis—two of which I still own today.

What can I say? That's wild… and a little embarrassing!

Epilogue

If in this story—my not-quite-novel, not-quite-autobiography—you find something that mirrors your own life, that's no coincidence. There's always a common thread, because God has a plan for each of us. It's been written since ancient times.

Up to this point, I believe I've shared a few interesting moments from my journey. I hope you smile at my written "madness" and enjoy reading the words of this apprentice writer. Yes, apprentice… even at my age! Hehehe.

My wish is that this story might encourage someone out there to write their own book or take on a new project—because when we tell our stories, we also inspire others to pursue their dreams.

And most importantly: thank God, I'm still alive. Today my life unfolds like that of most married older men—agreeing with everything my wife says. After forty years of marriage, she's no longer just "my woman," but truly my wife. And every time I answer that Lovely Girl, "Yes, ma'am—yes, ma'am," it reminds me of how I used to respond to the guards back in prison.

Oh, and to top it all off, that Lovely Girl now says she doesn't like me anymore… at this age!

Every car I've ever owned wasn't just a way to get around—it was a companion on the road through different chapters of my life. Some carried me to my first professional victories; others witnessed my mistakes and lessons learned. A few held my dreams, and others helped sustain my family through times of trial. Just as I changed vehicles, I too kept changing—traveling through straight roads and bumpy ones alike, but always with the deep certainty that, at the end of the journey, God has been my best co-pilot.

I just hope I don't end up with six more again....

www.ingramcontent.com/pod-product-compliance
Lightning Source LLC
Chambersburg PA
CBHW060515090426
42735CB00011B/2233